# DETENTE
# OR
# DEBACLE

# DETENTE
# OR
# DEBACLE

## Common Sense in
## U.S. - Soviet Relations

EDITED FOR THE AMERICAN COMMITTEE ON EAST-WEST ACCORD
AND WITH AN INTRODUCTION BY

Fred Warner Neal

Les Aspin • Stephen F. Cohen • Sidney D. Drell
John Kenneth Galbraith • Donald M. Kendall
George F. Kennan • G. B. Kistiakowsky
Samuel Pisar • David Riesman

Foreword by J. W. Fulbright

W · W · NORTON & COMPANY

NEW YORK

Copyright © 1979 by W. W. Norton & Company, Inc.
Published simultaneously in Canada by George J. McLeod Limited,
Toronto. Printed in the United States of America.
All Rights Reserved
First Edition

Library of Congress Cataloging in Publication Data
Main entry under title:

Detente or debacle.

1.   United States—Foreign relations—Russia—
Addresses, essays, lectures.   2.   Russia—Foreign
relations—United States—Addresses, essays, lectures.
3.   Detente—Addresses, essays, lectures.   I.   Neal,
Fred Warner.   II.   American Committee on East-West Accord.
E183.8.R9D47 1979     327.73'047     78-24092
ISBN 0-393-05706-2
ISBN 0-393-95008-5 pbk.

1 2 3 4 5 6 7 8 9 0

# NOTE

Many of the articles in *Detente or Debacle* were first brought together and printed in a limited edition by The American Committee on East-West Accord, an independent, nonpartisan, tax-exempt educational organization. The title of the American Committee book was *Common Sense in U.S.-Soviet Relations*.

Wide-spread interest in the subject of U.S.-Soviet relations and the competence of the authors encouraged the publication of a revised and up-dated version of the American Committee's book thereby making it available to a broader and different audience than was possible by private publication.

Each of the authors, with the exception of former Senator J. W. Fulbright and Congressman Les Aspin, is a member of the American Committee on East-West Accord.

Further information about the American Committee on East-West Accord may be obtained by writing to the national office in Washington: The American Committee on East-West Accord, 227 Massachusetts Ave., N.E., Suite 300, Washington, D.C. 20002.

# Contents

# Foreword

## J. W. Fulbright

The most difficult and the most important issue which will confront the American people during the next decade concerns our relations with the Soviet Union. It dwarfs all others because the Soviets as well as Americans are captive of an arms race which is out of control, a race which no one can win, a race in which increasingly exotic means of mutual and total destruction outrun diplomacy and can destroy the perspective and effectiveness of leadership in both nations.

While many Americans realize the arms race could end in utter disaster for both nations, attitudes on how to bring this race under control are becoming increasingly polarized and rigid. It is as outrageous to endorse the view that American security can only be achieved by increasing our strategic nuclear arsenal as it is to endorse the view that immediate unilateral disarmament is a sensible answer. It is these extremist views, however, which capture press attention and thereby harden the positions of extremists at both ends of the spectrum and in both the U.S. and Russia.

Neither American nor Soviet security can be found in these extremist views.

The articles in this book, which have been compiled by the American Committee on East-West Accord, are not those of extremists. The authors are experts and outstanding scholars of U.S.-Soviet relations. Their extensive experience reflected in the following analyses offers understanding, perspective and common sense.

None of the authors underestimate the significance of the different social, ideological or economic traditions of the two countries.

Americans believe their values — and way of life — is best for themselves and others. Conversely, Russians believe their social system is best for themselves and others. As a consequence, competition will continue between the superpowers in the years ahead as each system is tested in the marketplace of the searching and uncommitted.

It is essential that this competition be kept within the range of rationality so as to avoid the ultimate irrationality — mutual self-destruction through an all-out exchange of nuclear weapons.

The collection of articles in this booklet, *Common Sense in U.S.-Soviet Relations*, deserves the widest possible audience both here and in the Soviet Union.

*U. S. Senator (Dem., Ark.) 1945-1974; Chairman, Committee on Foreign Relations, U.S. Senate, 1959-1974.*

# INTRODUCTION
## By Fred Warner Neal

The most important issue facing the United States today concerns our relations with the Soviet Union. No single aspect of our society is unaffected by these relations — whether it be our economy, suffering from high military expenditures; our constitutional system, distorted by perceived requirements for national security; or, indeed, our very existence, ever threatened by expanding nuclear arsenals.

The vigorous efforts of both the United States and the Soviet Union to escape from three decades of Cold War and to build a more constructive relationship constituted the most hopeful development since the end of World War II. Out of these efforts emerged the beginnings of a detente aimed at establishing, through carefully negotiated, mutual agreements, that minimum of trust and cooperation necessary to insure coexistence.

It is not surprising that detente was a controversial issue from the start. There was throughout the land a deep and subconscious Cold War psychology. The Cold War had become a way of life for the United States. Numerous and powerful individuals and organizations had a stake in it — political, monetary, intellectual and emotional. A sharp break away from such a deeply entrenched set of beliefs and institutions was certain to produce a sharp reaction. Also, the most serious and complex issues of national security were involved. And, by no means least, the Nixon-Kissinger policy of detente was something new under the sun — the seeking of a network of treaties, agreements and understandings with a powerful and sometimes difficult adversary. Only Nixon, with his Eagle Scout anti-Communist credentials, aided by a brilliant master geopolitician like Kissinger, could have pulled it off.

"We cannot have the atmosphere of detente without the substance," Kissinger told the Russians, "but it is equally clear that the substance of detente will disappear in an atmosphere of hostility." In 1972, both atmosphere and substance improved almost at once. Moscow stopped its ideologically based attacks on the United States, and President Nixon ceased to engage in the militant anti-Communist rhetoric of his predecessors. The Voice of America, no longer jammed in the USSR, changed its previous strident hostile tone and content. Additionally, the

Fred Warner Neal is Executive Vice-President, American Committee on East-West Accord; Chairman, International Relations Faculty, Claremont Graduate School.

U.S. Navy quietly canceled the provocative "show the flag" movements which our warships had been making into the Black Sea; Soviet flotillas, which had made one foray into the Caribbean, now stayed out. Concomitantly, American businessmen in considerable numbers went to Moscow in anticipation of the new trade treaty, which called for Most Favored Nation status for the Soviet Union and multi-billion dollar credits from the Export-Import Bank.

On the surface detente seemed to be widely accepted. Nixon's authority as Mr. Conservative Republican was sufficient to keep the right wing of his party silent, if perplexed. His proposals for a larger military budget, detente or no detente, served to appease the Joint Chiefs of Staff and their claques in and out of Congress. And large sections of big business, interested in trade with the USSR as well as a more stable international climate, supported the new policy with unexpected enthusiasm.

Nevertheless, detente in fact began to falter almost as soon as it began. The events surrounding Watergate undermined Nixon's credibility and soon forced him from office. Senator Jackson, leading the American Jewish Community — or led by it — succeeded in blocking the trade agreement. President Ford decided that his struggle with Ronald Reagan for the Republican nomination barred any Presidential leadership on behalf of detente. The power and uncompromising positions of the military establishments and their civilian supporters in both the United States and the Soviet Union complicated progress on arms control. And differences between the Soviet and the Kissinger concepts of detente — e.g., Angola — subjected the new relationship to unexpected strains.

In spite of all this, on January 20, 1977, detente was still a viable policy. Although there was debate in this country about the nature of the Soviet commitment to detente, there was little question that the USSR strongly desired a continuing and expanded — if limited — cooperative relationship with the United States. What was needed to get detente back on the rails was primarily some new American initiative.

During the Carter Presidency, up to the summer of 1978, there has been no such initiative and no sign that one is planned. Where the Carter Administration has not acted as if American-Soviet relations were of secondary importance, or less, it has, intentionally or unintentionally, taken actions which have impeded progress toward detente. Our relationship with the USSR has, since 1972, been a peculiar sort of adversary-cooperative one. The Nixon-Ford Administrations emphasized the cooperative aspects. The Carter Administration has emphasized adversary aspects while doing little or nothing to improve the cooperative ones. And the President's National Security Adviser, Zbigniew Brzezinski, has over and over again urged a hard line — in the press, in TV talk shows and in such distant — if critical — places as the People's Republic of China.

The result was that by the summer of 1978 American-Soviet detente was in serious danger. The SALT negotiations, once thought to be on the verge of completion, stagnated. The dialogue established in 1972 had all but broken down. The Kremlin and the White House were talking past each other. Name-calling reminiscent of the Cold War began once more to characterize both sides. Both sides felt the other was to blame. American critics had many complaints about Soviet conduct. They focused — sometimes with considerable exaggeration — on the measured but steady build-up of Soviet armed forces, the Soviet/Cuban involvement in Africa, and the crackdown on dissidents inside the USSR.

If all this revealed differences in the American and the Soviet concepts of detente, it also indicated that detente was being overtaken by events. One of the aims of a detente relationship was to build mutual trust and cooperation to the point where the two sides could discuss their respective global interests in a business-like manner, where they could conclude agreements which would stop expansion of armed forces. To expect that these hoped-for results of detente could be achieved before the detente relationship was fully established was putting the cart before the horse. And as far as "human rights" in the USSR are concerned, a persuasive argument can be made that if they can be enlarged at all it is only in an atmosphere of detente. There is, in any event, no way in which the United States can force changes in the Soviet internal policies; indeed, the effort can be — and already has been — counterproductive. If instant democracy in the Soviet Union is an American requirement for detente, there clearly will be no detente.

In the various actions and pronouncements of the Carter Administration on these matters, the tone has been largely that of the anti-detente forces. If this resulted from domestic considerations, perhaps the President was listening to the wrong people. Certainly the critics of detente have dominated the news media with their cries about Soviet perfidy and the danger of American softness. Despite this, however, a Harris Poll in the spring of 1978 found that a 71-14 majority favors "detente — that is, the United States and Russia seeking out areas of agreement and cooperation." The question arises, why this majority opinion has been so largely ignored by the Carter Administration? Was it not there, waiting only to be rallied by Presidential leadership?

Arguments favoring this majority opinion are too rarely heard. Yet they have been forthcoming from important segments of society, as evidenced by this book.

This book, put together at the initiative of the American Committee on East-West Accord, sets forth moderate, objective, expert opinions of distinguished Americans, based on realistic concern for the best interest of the United States. The broad political scope of the American Committee is indicated by its co-chairmen — George F. Kennan, John Kenneth Galbraith, and Donald M. Kendall. The Committee is a remarkable non-partisan group of private citizens — corporation executives, former ambassadors, college presidents, Soviet specialists, nuclear physicists, clergymen of all faiths — who differ widely among themselves about politics, economics, and international affairs. They are, however, united in believing that a common-sense workable relationship with the Soviet Union is not only vital for our national interest but also possible to achieve.

All the authors represented in the present book — with the exceptions of Congressman Aspin and former Senator Fulbright — are members of the American Committee on East-West Accord and represent its general point of view. They do not anticipate that U.S.-Soviet relations, at best, will be a love feast. They are conscious that there are fundamental differences dividing the two societies which are unlikely to be overcome. They do not believe in compromising basic American interests. They stress the importance of keeping our powder dry, and comparatively plentitudinous. They are firm in their conviction that detente should never be — as it has not been — a one-way street for either side. Yet they reflect a conviction that on this basis we can work out a relationship with the Soviet Union which serves recognizable mutual interests as well as the interests of the world at large. They also reflect a conviction that we must do so, for the future of all of us, and our civilization, depends upon it.

The essays that follow rebut, point by point, most of the arguments made by critics of detente. They urge greater recognition of the fact that Soviet society itself has changed since Stalin's time and continues to change, generally in ways favorable to a better relationship with the United States. They express the view that we can best encourage wider political freedom in the Soviet Union through an atmosphere of detente and that the Carter "human rights" approach is both self-defeating and harmful to American Soviet relations. They contend that eliminating trade discrimination against the Soviet Union would produce a more cooperative relationship generally as well as increases in Jewish emigration. And they put the question of relative American and Soviet military strength in needed perspective. Criticizing "doomsday scenarios" and "worst case" analyses of Soviet military posture, they warn that only by SALT agreements based on parity and leading to arms reduction can we achieve security and hope for the future. In all this, the authors reflect a sense of urgency, echoing Henry Kissinger's admonition in his *Pacem in Terris* address that "opportunities cannot be hoarded; once past, they are usually irretrievable."

# DETENTE
# OR
# DEBACLE

# LET'S PUT DETENTE BACK ON THE RAILS

## By Samuel Pisar

The direction President Carter takes in his dealings with the Kremlin will predetermine the state of American-Soviet relations — and hence the lot of mankind — for a decade ahead. Attitudes that control the way great powers act and react toward each other cannot be shifted back and forth from year to year. Therefore, it is of paramount importance that we consider now where we are going and where we will end up.

By making human rights the center-piece of his foreign policy, the President has rehabilitated the tarnished American image of the Vietnam and Watergate years and has placed the United States where it belongs — in the forefront of the fight for freedom and justice. But his crusade to liberalize Communist societies through external pressure has had to be toned down. For in pursuing a venture in morality whose chances of success were questionable, to say the least, other vital objectives — above all the hope of defusing the perilous military rivalry between the super-powers — were being jeopardized and American-Soviet relations were sinking to their lowest point in years.

Whether, as a nation, we should or should not seek to advance the dignity of man everywhere is not in question. The American people like their foreign policy to project a clear moral purpose. Henry Kissinger, rooted in Metternich's pragmatism, did not cater to this reality. Jimmy Carter read the country's mood more accurately. By offering a more idealistic, more confident view of America's role in the world, he has broadened the base of public support for a new foreign policy. But in the process the task of addressing urgent global problems that cannot be resolved without active East-West cooperation has been slowed.

*Samuel Pisar is an international lawyer and a noted authority on American-Soviet trade. A former adviser to the State Department and to the Joint Economic Committee of Congress, he is the author of Coexistence and Commerce. The article below is based on one which appeared in The New York Times Magazine Sept. 25, 1977.*

Against this background, Carter's early positions on strategic arms, on the cruise missile, on the neutron bomb, and on increased Allied contributions to NATO's military budget, acquires the appearance of escalation. Inevitably, one issue has become politically and psychologically linked to another. The result is virtual suspension of progress toward an understanding, even where the United States and the Soviet Union have a clear community of interest. Reciprocal plans to slow down the arms race are put on the back burner. Trade stagnates because corporate executives, uncertain of the political situation, hold back on new transactions. Even more, businessmen, scientists, artists, and others involved in economic, technical and cultural exchanges fall prey to a guilt complex, as they are made to feel they are supping with the devil.

## A Hazardous Enterprise

In and of themselves, the President's words and gestures in regard to the sorry state of human rights in the Soviet Union hardly justify the chorus of complaints from Moscow. His personal letter to the distinguished Russian scientist and dissident Andrei Sakharov was little more than an offer of compassion. The same can be said of his meeting at the White House with the dissident emigre Vladimir Bukovsky; if that meeting appeared provocative, it was largely because of President Ford's somewhat inept refusal to receive Aleksandr Solzhenitsyn two years earlier. Carter's decision to expand the operations of Radio Free Europe and Radio Liberty can be attributed to a desire to promote the flow of information, now that Russia has agreed to stop jamming Western broadcasts. Cumulatively, however, this succession of statements and actions creates a militant atmosphere. Leading Administration figures then transmute the atmosphere into intellectual doctrine.

To force the pace of reconciliation between former adversaries, as Nixon and Brezhnev sought to do at their meetings in 1972 and 1973, is a hazardous enterprise. It is equally hazardous, however, to reduce the momentum on grounds that tend to dehumanize the opponent and reawaken public antagonisms. Both in Russia and in America, popular memory holds on to the grim scenario of cold-war crises that began to unfold in the late 1940's. The traumas this scenario has engendered are easily revived in a nation's psyche, and are not easily laid to rest. If not handled with care, the fragile thaw that came into Soviet-American relations in the last five years could freeze over again.

There are powerful groups in both countries that would welcome such a development. Soviet critics of detente complain that the Soviet Union has lost its position in the Middle East; that the Helsinki accords have bred subversive ideas in Eastern Europe; that America has raised the ante in the strategic-arms negotiations; that the United States Congress presumes to legislate on the U.S.S.R.'s internal affairs, and that the big trade breakthrough has not materialized. American critics point to the harsh treatment of Russia's dissidents and minority groups; Moscow's intervention in Angola and the Horn of Africa by Cuban proxy; to Soviet overreaching in the notorious American wheat deal, and to the massive buildup of the Russian army and navy at a time when, in these critic's view, the West is being lulled into a false sense of security.

Even among those who favor detente, mistrust on both sides runs deep, for serious and legitimate concerns loom in the background. But a way must be found to break out of the vicious circle — to overcome the paralysis of fear that seizes one side as it speculates endlessly on the hidden motives of the other.

It is always difficult to draw a clear line between style and substance in the conduct of foreign affairs. From years of extensive and often difficult negotiations with the Russians, I have come to believe that, in Soviet-American relations, style and substance are inseparable.

The recent moral posturing in Washington has baffled Moscow (and, for that matter, most other capitals in Eastern and Western Europe as well.) The old guard that still holds power in the Kremlin can't figure out if we are deliberately stepping on their most sensitive corns or doing so out of sheer clumsiness; in either case, their capacity for political cooperation is reduced. The younger and more moderate groups waiting in the wings are also confused as to whether we want to play ball with them or go for their jugular. Whether these perceptions are justified or not is secondary. The danger is that Russia's hawks, eternally preoccupied with military security and ideological purity, will seize upon these renewed suspicions to bring the process of detente to a halt. That could trigger a similar spasm on our side. It is not difficult to imagine a sudden return to the tensions of the late 40's and 50's. The world is replete with potential trouble spots. Either side could easily make life difficult for the other.

## Moral Aspects of Detente

The moral aspects of detente are obviously delicate. Instinctively, we cannot help being moved by the fearless plea of the Russian dissidents that the lofty words of the Soviet Constitution, the Helsinki agreement and the Universal Declaration on Human Rights be given meaningful expression in the policies and practices of the Soviet state. We must also bear in mind however, that in Russia, since time immemorial, the quest for freedom as we know it has never progressed beyond a dream. Solzhenitsyn's message today is a delayed echo of Patrick Henry's cry, "Give me liberty or give me death." In a thermonuclear age, this echo, stirringly though it still rings in our ears, cannot receive a purely emotional response.

Surely no rational observer can doubt by now that both Eastern Communism and Western democracy will survive into the indefinite future. Neither side will voluntarily dismantle its institutions or be forced to do so by the other side. The critical question is how to move the contest between them from the shadow of mutual annihilation to the arena of constructive coexistence.

The new Administration's approach to this problem does not appear to have been firmly set. Those who favor a foreign policy with a strong emphasis on human rights — an outlook that has found an articulate theoretician in the President's top national-security adviser, Zbigniew Brzezinski — represent one tendency, hitherto in control. Others on the team appear to take somewhat different views. Secretary of State Cyrus Vance seemed to hint at his discomfort when he said recently that "in pursuing a human-rights policy, we must always keep in mind the limits of our power and of our wisdom." Carter himself has admitted, with characteristic candor, that the Russians' reaction to his position on human rights took him by surprise and "constituted a greater obstacle to common goals like SALT than I had anticipated." Will we now have to pay a higher price in negotiation over substance because the irritations over style have poisoned the climate of confidence built up by previous Administrations? This question will hang omniously over the next round of Soviet-American contacts. We seem, in fact, to be at a crossroads.

Personally, I believe that to link the normalization of relations to fundamental changes in the Soviets' internal system, and to do so openly and aggressively, is to undermine the remnants of detente — and, at the same time, to bury the prospect of expanded human rights in the Soviet Union. In answer to a series of questions I put to him publicly in 1973, Andrei Sakharov answered me in the world press: "I am unconditionally against ultimatums of any kind in relations between states . . . . I am in favor of the gradual improvement of the Soviet state within the framework of the existing regime." The only challenge that promises to liberalize that regime is a commitment to engage its less fanatical elements in a constructive dialogue of cooperation, with expanded commercial, technological and scientific intercourse as the central theme. This approach, based on our vastly superior capacity for economic progress, and on the human freedoms that inexorably go with it, is in the mainstream of the American ethic.

I agree with Sakharov, who knows the situation intimately from the inside, that the true remedy for Russia's chronic agricultural and industrial ills lies in democratic reforms and the progressive integration of the Soviet economy into the world market. If the U.S.S.R. is not to become a second-rate power, it will have to experiment with new concepts of production, distribution and management. Such experimentation is inseparable from freedom of expression and communications, both at home and abroad.

If the historian Amalrik cannot write, if the cellist Rostropovich cannot play, if the dancer Panov cannot dance, if the scientist Levich cannot teach, then the technician cannot really innovate, the engineer cannot produce and the manager cannot manage. In an age of galloping technological change, there can be no sustained economic progress unless minds are free. This is the lesson of our own national experience and, in the truest sense, our message to the world. It should be at the heart of our policy toward the East.

New beginnings based on this more hopeful vision of coexistence were made in the early days of the Kennedy Administration. Eager to test the Russian's readiness to do business, the President wanted to know what enticing signal he might send to Moscow. His task force on foreign economic policy, on which I served at the time, recommended that he abolish the American embargo on Soviet crabmeat, imposed because it was allegedly produced with slave labor. This was, in fact, a response to an earlier gambit made by Chairman Khrushchev while de-Stalinizing his regime. Always ahead of his time, Khrushchev climbed onto an improvised platform in the Soviet pavillion at the 1959 Leipzig fair, introduced himself with humor as "the representative of the business circles of the U.S.S.R." and announced to the assembled captains of Western industry that his clients were in the market for equipment, patents and know-how.

The Bay of Pigs, the Cuban missile crisis and Kennedy's assassination interrupted this dialogue. It took a decade of patient effort on both sides to re-establish a favorable atmosphere. Those of us who were directly involved in the effort were not blind to the risks and difficulties that lurked in a more open economic policy toward the East. Many delicate questions had to be resolved. What ground rules would be appropriate in expanded transactions between a state-enterprise and free-enterprise system? How could an open, competitive economy such as ours deal safely and securely with a secret, state-operated economy such as theirs? How could the flow of truly strategic equipment and technology be effectively controlled? Most of all how could we, in good conscience, be indifferent to the argument of some of the dissidents that broadened commerce would only strengthen the Soviet Government's dictatorial grip on the people? While these questions were being pondered and agonized over, something positive began happening, something that opened up new perspectiveness for peace and freedom.

As goods, people and ideas began to cross the East-West boundary in an atmosphere of receding tension, intellectual ferment of a kind not seen since the early years of the Bolshevik Revolution began to make itself felt in Russia and other parts of the Soviet bloc. In Poland and Czechoslovakia, in particular, alienated groups were emboldened to voice their discontent. In Hungary, the regime itself instituted significant economic and political reforms.

## The Jackson-Vanik Amendment

These admittedly tenuous but promising beginnings ran into the Jackson-Vanik amendment of 1974, which tied normalization of trade with Moscow to freer emigration of Soviet Jews. Stung by what it regarded as humiliating interference in its internal affairs, the Soviet Government abrogated the Soviet-American trade agreement of 1972. The well-intentioned Jackson-Vanik amendment proved ineffective, if not counter-productive. On this we now have a full and depressing record.

Throughout the ages, minority groups, and Jews in particular, have been among the first victims of severe international tensions. It was the relaxation of East-West tensions that permitted more than 100,000 Jews to depart from the Soviet Union, and comparable numbers to leave Eastern Europe, in the last 10 years. While thousands more are clamoring to emigrate, and simple humanity demands that everyone have the right to leave his country if he so chooses, the evolving emigration patterns were at least a start, compared with the hermetically sealed borders of the Stalinist era. Jewish emigration began to reach significant numbers in the early 70's. Fewer than 1,000 visas were issued in 1970, but in 1971, according to both Soviet and American sources, the figure jumped to around 15,000. It rose again in 1972, to around 30,000 and it reached a peak of around 35,000 in 1973. By the end of 1974, when debate on the Jackson-Vanik amendment was at its height, the annual rate had declined to around 20,000. Following passage of the amendment, the figure fell further — to less than 15,000 in 1975 and about the same in 1976.

In retrospect, Kissinger's quieter brand of diplomacy on this sensitive issue appears to have been more fruitful. The same is true of the discreet diplomatic approach chosen by Chancellor Schmidt; last year, he managed to obtain the repatriation of 70,000 ethnic Germans from the Soviet bloc. Carefully modulated external pressure can indeed be productive, but public, official attempts to coerce a proud power are generally self-defeating.

Today, trade and emigration remain enmeshed in complicated stalemate. The delicate task of reactivating both will require wisdom and forbearance in Washington as well as in Moscow. A significant increase in emigration would speak more eloquently than any formal diplomatic understanding, and nothing could demonstrate better to the American Congress and the American people that the insertion of politically embarrassing conditions into our trade legislation was not necessary in the first place.

The lingering view of many policy makers that a Western refusal to trade will dislocate or force open the Communist world, or at least compel it to divert resources from strategic to civilian pursuits, is far too simplistic. (Khruschev used to quip that America should not sell to Russia that most strategic commodity of all, ordinary buttons, because, with buttons on their pants, Soviet Army soldiers can aim their rifles with both hands instead of one.) In fact, it is far from certain that our own democratic system can withstand a destabilizing defense budget in excess of $100 billion more easily than our authoritarian adversaries. A deteriorating balance of payments, rising energy costs, declining educational standards, rampant poverty among blacks, and a host of other problems that fester for lack of funds, threaten to undermine our society

6

from the inside. Western Europe and Japan, faced with a comparable choice of priorities between military and civilian needs, have long ago opted for the axiom that security, like charity, begins at home.

To the present generation of Soviet leaders, those who have fought and suffered in the war against the Nazis, the choice between guns and butter is considerably less difficult than we tend to believe. Their paranoid preoccupation with security, stemming as it does from recurrent historical experience, causes them to sacrifice the consumer without too much risk or regret. A population whose memories of invasion from the west are still painfully fresh can endure hardship with surprising stoicism. Today, that population is subject to the added fear of a growing threat from China. I recall how, at a high-level Soviet-American meeting in Kiev in July 1971, our eminent Soviet hosts, including Georgi Arbatov, the Kremlin's foremost adviser on American affairs, could hardly contain their consternation when the news broke that Kissinger had just completed a secret mission to Peking.

For the younger of the Soviet elite who are now on the threshold of power, the allocation of scarce resources between an insatiable military machine and the most elementary requirements of the long-suffering population is, however, a painful dilemma indeed. This generation is bored with the stories of wartime heroism that condition the bemedaled old men who still hold the levers of authority. Their interest is in the future. Like the millions of young Americans who are worried about the chaos in our urban centers, the growth of violent crime, the persistence of unemployment and inflation and the deterioration of the environment, these younger Russians are primarily concerned with urgent domestic issues. They are preoccupied with technological backwardness, housing shortages, labor inefficiency, alcoholism and the chronic inadequacy of Soviet agriculture. It is a safe bet that they do not want to sacrifice forever, on the altar of a stale ideology, their hope of more freedom and a better standard of life, much less to run the risk of an apocalyptic showdown with the West.

## A Workable Equation of Coexistence

If they are prepared to build automobiles, highways, filling stations, parking lots, motels and roadside restaurants, it is in our own interest to help them along. With time, they can be expected to become a more mobile, more complex and more peaceful society. The benefits of our cooperation will go to their system's midriff rather than to its biceps.

As the Communist East strains under the burden of excessive political and economic regimentation, and as the liberal West braces itself for the onslaught of social disorder, both have much to gain from expanded contacts, and each has something to learn from the other. This is a workable equation for coexistence.

Even those in the East who still subscribe to the established dogma know that hard choices lie ahead. If they do not allow the warm winds of Western know-how to blow eastward, they will continue to be faced, year after year, with stagnant industry and agriculture. On the other hand, if they loosen up their system, they may unleash changes that will sweep away their totalitarian power. I believe that the social and economic pressures within the Soviet Union are sufficiently strong to tip the balance in favor of those willing to relax the iron grip. Coercion from the outside will only render their task more difficult and push them deeper into the arms of the hard-liners, who remain forever poised for the ultimate test of strength.

Paradoxically, America's historical experience is becoming more and more relevant to Russia's present needs. Despite the deep political gulf that still separates them, the two countries have great affinities, especially those of scale. Both are continent-sized, and both have vast populations, endless seacoasts, mighty rivers, diverse climates and enormous natural resources. The challenge facing Russia's leaders today is one of providing decent living standards for their people. That America has met this challenge like no previous society is not lost on the rising generation of frustrated Soviet planners, managers and technicians. To observe the enthusiasm of these people at an audio-visual presentation by American experts on how citrus fruit is grown in the swamps of Florida, how lipstick is manufactured in the industrial centers of New Jersey or how tractors are operated in the praries of Oklahoma, is to see human beings immersed in the process of creation, indifferent to the dogmatic pretensions of Marxism-Lenisnism. Those who are engaged in this process have demonstrated a startling fact — that they can cross national and ideological frontiers between East and West more effectively than armies, churches or diplomats.

When like-minded people of this kind become mobilized by common goals, the web of relationships they weave — industry to industry, enterprise to enterprise, man to man — is more difficult to tear up than the most ambitiously conceived diplomatic arrangement. For they are staking their careers and their future on the constructive projects in which they participate. Because they want these projects to survive and prosper, they are a force for stability, a growing counterweight to the metal eaters who remain addicted, on both sides, to the endless expansion of their military arsenals. This human dimension of detente is bound to increase pressures within the Soviet system for the satisfaction of other aspirations that have been sacrificed thus far.

Beyond their mutual relations, both East and West have immense worldwide problems that, from any rational standpoint, eclipse their continuing disagreements. Energy and raw-material shortages, the pollution of the atmosphere and the oceans, the gap between population growth and food supply, the erosion of the established monetary system and the weakness of international organizations — to say nothing of the awesome proliferation of nuclear arms — threaten all countries indiscriminately, be they rich or poor, large or small, communist or capitalist. On all these issues, America and Russia share a community of interest. To respond to the common fears and common needs that assail both nations, novel forms of cooperation must be given an opportunity to emerge.

## The Energy Crisis

The world energy crisis is a case in point. Recent C.I.A. studies show that while Russia today sells more oil to the West than to its own allies, by 1985 — precisely when America, Western Europe and Japan will face disruptive and possibly catastrophic shortages — the Soviet block will need to import an additional 5 million barrels of oil per day. The opening of proven Siberian wells and of the abundant sources of natural gas, coal and hydroelectric power east of the Urals would avert this need and bring significant new supplies to the world market.

Whether American industry should be encouraged to participate in the development of Siberia's energy resources is a ticklish political question. But on economic grounds, such participation would make eminent sense. It would ease the mounting pressure on world prices, help us diversify our unhealthy dependence on the Middle East and improve our trade balance, insofar as Russian export earnings may be expected to go to increased purchases of American goods. It is often overlooked that, in the last few years, this balance has been running, by hundreds of millions of dollars, in our favor.

In the summer of 1973, I discussed these possibilities with that veteran Bolshevik leader Anastas Mikoyan. Himself an expert on trade matters, Mikoyan spoke of the U.S.S.R.'s readiness to market liquefied natural gas to the West. "We would not be willing to sell you more than a fraction of this wealth," he told me, "because your energy problems today are ours tomorrow, and our children and grandchildren will not forgive us for depleting the vital fuel sources they will need one day to light and heat Moscow, Leningrad and Kiev." He admitted, however, that "because we need your equipment and, periodically, your surplus grain to feed our people, we must sell whatever we can to earn the hard currency with which to pay you."

The deepening poverty of the underdeveloped world is another case in point. In recent years, experimental groups of Western private enterprise and Communist state enterprise have become active in certain countries of Africa and Asia. If this trend were to pick up momentum, many desperate regions could be converted from sterile theaters of political and military confrontation into stabler and more productive areas of joint enterprise. I have heard Russians wonder aloud how many billions of rubles their Government has squandered, without any lasting diplomatic benefit, on military aid to Egypt and the construction of the Aswan Dam. Had that last project been undertaken jointly by the United States and the Soviet Union, rather than in the spirit of a spectacular propaganda contest

9

fanned by President Nasser, the results would have been more satisfactory technically, ecologically and economically. Today, many an American might wonder whether the same futile contest will characterize the superpowers' relationship in India and Africa, or whether something useful will at last be done for hundreds of millions of people perpetually on the verge of famine.

## Needed: A Resolute Push

The Carter Administration has put urgent tasks on mankind's agenda, among them the limitation on strategic arms, the control of nuclear proliferation and the construction of a new system of world relations. These goals will remain unattainable so long as the two superpowers remain locked in acrimonious wrangle over the moral parameters of detente. Unless both sides pull back from ideological hostilities whose only effect is to exacerbate tensions on all fronts, mankind will sink ever deeper into military confrontation, political terrorism and social chaos.

Statements recently made by President Carter and President Brezhnev indicate that neither side wants to push the present tensions to the breaking point. But a mere standoff will not revive the dynamic of understanding that was painstakingly built up in recent years. What is needed is a resolute push by both leaders to bring the bogged-down schedule of negotiations back to life.

On the eve of the changing of the Kremlin guard, the United States has a historic opportunity to lay stable foundations for constructive East-West coexistence. The moment is uniquely propitious for letting the younger generation of Soviet leaders know we are ready to proceed with them toward new vistas of bilateral and global cooperation.

It is through practical deeds in the sphere of science, technology, industry and commerce, where basic interests coincide and ideological differences recede, that each side can put its best foot forward. Expanded economic intercourse, mutually advantageous in itself, can serve as a powerful impetus to a general accommodation. This evolutionary process offers the best hope of expanding human freedom and dignity everywhere — and of attaining our own national objectives, at home as well as abroad.

The common concern for survival and prosperity requires that this process go forward.

# SOVIET DOMESTIC POLITICS AND FOREIGN POLICY

## By Stephen F. Cohen

S oviet Russia has been on our minds — a virtual obsession — for exactly sixty years. During these sixty years, far more has changed in the Soviet Union, and in the world, than in our perceptions and ideas. Even now, as a new American debate on Soviet domestic and foreign policy unfolds, it seems clear that much of our thinking still bears deep traces of that narrow consensus once admired as "bipartisanship," and that in many quarters cold-war attitudes and misconceptions are as firmly lodged as ever. This should alarm us, not only because of the sterile foreign policies this kind of thinking once produced, but because of the way these cold-war attitudes have distorted our own domestic values and priorities.

Any rethinking about Soviet intentions and behavior abroad must begin with an understanding of Soviet domestic politics and society. Indeed, American thinking about Soviet foreign policy over the years has almost always emphasized this connection; and, by the same token, most of our misconceptions of Soviet intentions abroad have derived from misconceptions of the character and direction of Soviet domestic factors. In particular, the tenacious view of a continuously revolutionary and militantly expansionist Soviet Union, a view that dominated American thinking for so long and has now, after a short decline, reappeared in opposition to detente, is based on a static, ahistorical image of a fundamentally unchanged and unchanging Soviet system. Just as observed alterations in Soviet foreign policy are dismissed, in this view, as merely tactical maneuvers in a relentless drive for world conquest, so too are internal changes said to be secondary to the basic continuities that determine the real nature of the Soviet Union and its intentions abroad.

No informed person will deny that the Soviet political system continues to be a highly authoritarian and often repressive one, which systematically

*Dr. Cohen is Director of the Russian Studies Program and Associate Professor of Politics at Princeton University. His contribution here is based on a statement made in October 1977 to a Subcommittee of the House Committee on International Relations. It first appeared in* Inquiry Magazine, *December 19, 1977.*

deprives its citizens of elementary political liberties, or that the USSR is a formidable international adversary with great power ambitions around the world. Nor will a careful student any longer argue either of two once-popular extremes—that there is an immutable irreconcilability between the Soviet Union and the United States; or, on the other hand, that modern history is somehow moving toward a "convergence" between the two systems. The rejection of these two excessive perspectives should be our starting point, the minimal consensus from which different perspectives proceed. Beyond this, however, there is an almost unlimited potential for disagreement among knowledgeable people.

We have learned a great deal about Soviet life in recent years, but this knowledge has demonstrated mainly that none of our conceptions or models of the Soviet Union are adequate — that all are far too simplistic. The main thing we have learned is that behind the crumbling facade of political and social conformity, there is a tremendous diversity and complexity of reality at every level of Soviet life. Students of Soviet economics, for example, have begun to speak less of an omnipotent centralized planned economy and more of a "multicolored" economy of official and unofficial components, state and private enterprises, controlled and free transactions, of red, white, grey, and black markets.[1] We need the same kind of "multi-colored" approach to Soviet reality in general, which conforms as little to our models as it does to official Soviet ones, whether we are discussing the high politics of the Communist Party or the everyday life of ordinary citizens.

In this connection, I want to make four very general points about Soviet politics and society. They concern realities often obscured but which influence Soviet intentions and behavior abroad in important ways. First, the history of the Soviet Union provides many examples of internal change, and there is no reason to exclude the possibility of further change in the future. Second, the Soviet leadership today faces—as will its successor—an array of serious domestic and foreign problems; and while these problems should not be construed as crises that seriously enfeeble or endanger the system, neither should they be minimized. Third, there is within both Soviet society and the establishment itself a great diversity of opinion, political outlook, and proposed solutions to these problems. And fourth, this diversity of opinion must nonetheless be understood in the general context of a deep rooted political and social conservatism, which is widespread among Soviet officials and ordinary citizens alike.

## Change in the Soviet System

To understand that Soviet history has witnessed periodic and far-reaching internal changes is to reject the popular view of an immutable Soviet system. The fact that the main institutions of the political system — the Communist Party, the official Marxist-Leninist ideology, the planned state economy, the political police, and so forth — have continued to exist over the years says little. It is a commonplace of political history that deep changes in the working and nature of a political system often occur within a continuous institutional framework, and in this process the institutions themselves are inwardly changed. The American Presidency and the English Parliament continue to exist; but they are not the same institutions they were in the 19th century. Nor do the American and English political systems function just as they did a hundred years ago. Even the names that historians customarily give to the main periods in Soviet political history bespeak the deep changes that have recurred since 1917: War Communism, the New Economic Policy, Stalinization, de-Stalinization.

The most recent of these great changes in the Soviet Union must be kept in mind when we talk about the present and and the future. Our focus on the continuing authoritarianism and political abuses in the Soviet Union obscures the fact that during the Khrushchev years there occurred in that country an authentic political and social reformation. Virtually every area of Soviet life was affected by the changes, however contradictory and ultimately limited, of 1953-1964, from the end of mass terror and freeing of millions of prison camp victims, the measures introduced to limit at least some of the worst bureaucratic abuses and privileges, the civic awakening and growing political participation of educated society, and the array of economic and welfare reforms, to revisions in Soviet foreign policy that led to what we now call detente.

For our own thinking, the significance of this reformation (sometimes called de-Stalinization), which changed the Soviet Union for the better in many fundamental ways, is threefold. First, it reminds us that current Soviet abuses of power and violations of civil rights, however deplorable, are far more limited and less severe than in the Stalinist past. Second, it is evidence that a short time ago there existed inside the Soviet Union, within the Soviet political establishment, and apart from international pressures, significant forces for reform. There is no reason to assume that such forces do not still exist. And third, it helps us to understand the conservative reaction that followed the overthrow of Khrushchev in 1964 and continues today. In another society, this reaction would be considered normal. In American and English politics, for example, it is thought to be virtually axiomatic that periods of reform are followed by conservative backlashes.

Some of the major problems faced by the Soviet leadership today are common to industrial societies, but many are the direct legacy of Soviet historical development, the limitations of the reforms of 1953-1964, and the conservative reaction after 1964. Western specialists disagree as to which problems are the most serious, much depending on the specialist's own interests. Suffice it to itemize a few that Soviet citizens themselves emphasize.

At home, there is a chronic decline in industrial and technological development and persistently low labor productivity; a collective agricultural system which still cannot reliably feed the population; widespread consumer grumbling and housing shortages; a politically restive intellectual class; disenchantment with official values among young people; growing birth rates and nationalist sentiments among the major non-Slav groups, and a declining birth rate among Russians; a small but defiant dissident movement along with a large readership of uncensored (*samizdat*) literature; and, in the realm of political authority, the still unresolved, and pertinent, question of the terrible crimes of the Stalin era. More generally, I would stress the overarching administrative problem of a centralized bureaucratic system created in the very different conditions of the 1930's, which still prevails in all areas of Soviet life — political, economic, social, cultural, scientific — and which generates and institutionalizes a multitude of inefficiencies, Catch 22's, and popular resentments. On another level, I would stress the manifestations of rampant alcoholism and family disintegration, and, from the party's viewpoint, the revival of religious belief, because they reflect or impinge upon so many other problems.

At the same time, the Soviet leadership, for all its gains as a great power since 1945, can find little solace in foreign policy achievements. There is the perceived menace of China; the recalcitrant empire in Eastern Europe, which has been the scene of a major crisis every decade; the advent in Western Europe of so-called Euro-communist parties, whose success threatens to complete the de-Russification of international communism; the familiar problem of third-world "allies," who become fickle or difficult to control, as in Egypt and India; and the staggering costs of a global competition, however, peaceful, with the United States.

The main thing to be said about these problems is not that they portend an imminent crisis, but that they represent long-term and hopelessly intertwined dilemmas and impose severe constraints on domestic and foreign policy, and that there is no real majority view as to their solution.[2] In part, this is because no majority consensus has been allowed to develop through an uncensored public discussion. But, equally, it is because of the deep divisions on every major issue and problem, even among Soviet officials and party members.

For many years, misled by the silence and conformity imposed by Stalin's terror, we imagined something that did not exist — a homogeneous Soviet officialdom and even society. The complex reality is now clear: the diversity of Soviet opinion is probably equal to that in any "open" society (though more private, of course), ranging from orthodox Marxism-Leninism to Russian Orthodox religion, from democratic to authoritarian, liberal to neo-fascist, from left to right. More important for our purposes, variations of this diversity exist within the political establishment and even inside the ruling Communist Party.

This will surprise those who take seriously official claims of a "monolithic" party, who continue to speak meaninglessly of "the

Soviets," "the Communist mind," and "ideological blueprints," and who imagine an unbridgeable gulf between the party-state and society-at-large. In fact, it may be that a monopolistic political party inescapably acquires a more diverse membership than do parties in multiparty systems simply because there is no organized alternative.[3] Whatever the case, it makes no sense to think of the Communist Party, with its more than 15 million members, or the Soviet state, which employs virtually the entire population, as somehow remote or apart from society. At the very least, we must understand that while the party-state seeks to direct and control society, it is permeated by the diverse, conflicting attitudes of that society.

It is in this context that we can gain a better perspective on the dissident movement, which has come to figure so prominently in American thinking and, alas, is in danger of becoming the hostage of our foreign policy. Western specialists have trouble reconciling two seemingly con-tradictory truths. On the one hand, we know that the emergence and per-sistence of open dissent is an important development in Soviet history. On the other hand, we know that the active dissidents are very small in numbers and political impact.

How can we reconcile these truths? By realizing, I think, that most of the different trends of thought expressed openly by dissidents are to be found, in at least some subterranean form, within Soviet officialdom. This does not mean that dissident activists are spokesmen for real or potential oppositionists inside the establishment, but simply that dissident views reflect in significant measure, however obliquely, the array, and disarray of attitudes among officials as well.

Most important for our thinking about future Soviet and American policy are the competing political trends inside the Communist Party, and particularly at its middle and upper levels. Our knowledge here is im-precise, and this advises caution and against speculation. But it is safe to say that the three main trends, which have formed and struggled over the past 25 years, may be termed reformist, conservative, and reactionary or neo-Stalinist.[4] I use these terms loosely to designate amalgams of party opinion, not single-minded groupings.

Party reformers, who are certainly now the weakest in number and in-fluence, include some advocates of authentic democratization, but many more administrators, managers, or technocrats who only want more in-itiative, and hence some liberalization, in their own areas of responsibility, be it the economy, science, culture, or international affairs. The conser-vatives, who have predominated almost everywhere in Soviet politics since the mid-1960's, also include various types, from sincere believers in the virtues of the *status quo* to cynical defenders of vested bureaucratic interests. Some lean toward the moderate reformers, some toward the neo-Stalinists. The party's neo-Stalinist wing can only be called reactionary. Its solutions to contemporary problems are couched in an extreme Rus-sian chauvinism and nostalgia for the more despotic ways of the Stalin days, though short of the mass terror which, as they know, victimized

Soviet officials capriciously, regardless of political outlook.

Although these party trends are part of the power struggles that range more or less continuously across all the important policy areas, it would be wrong to think that they have nothing in common. All are proud of the Soviet Union's achievements at home and abroad, nationalistic and patriotic in one way or another, loyal to the party system, and, to take a specific example, fearful about China. Nor are they incapable of collaboration in various areas of policy-making. Like politics elsewhere, much of Soviet politics involves compromises and coalitions. Most reformers and conservatives seem now to favor, for example, detente and expanding economic relations with the West, though for different reasons; reformers hope it will promote economic reform at home, while conservatives hope it will enable them to avoid it. At the same time, there has been a growing conservative-neo-Stalinist coalition in cultural and intellectual policy in recent years.

Future change in the Soviet Union will depend in large measure on the struggle between these trends in the party. Change can be for the better or the worse, of course, toward liberalization or back toward a harsher authoritarianism. Since its inception in 1964, and especially since 1966-68, the conservative or centrist, Brezhnev government has turned increasingly toward the party's neo-Stalinist wing, particularly in domestic affairs. The bleak prospect of still greater neo-Stalinist influence, or even a leadership dominated by these party elements, cannot be excluded. I personally, however, have not yet succumbed to the chronic pessimism that seems eventually to come over many Western Specialists on the Soviet Union. I do not rule out the possibility of another wave of reform, during or in the aftermath of a leadership succession.

## Soviet Reform and Conservatism

Any genuine reform requires, however, two conditions, both of which concern us. First, it must be reform with a Soviet face. Those among us who argue that Soviet reform must be patterned on Western examples or imposed from abroad understand little about Russia or the process of reform in general. No reform movement anywhere, but especially in a country as historically self-conscious as the Soviet Union, can be successful estranged from its own history and culture. It must find inspiration, roots, and ultimately legitimacy within its native — in this case, Russian and Soviet — political and historical traditions. A Soviet reformism couched in Westernism, or encumbered by foreign sponsors, would be tainted and doomed. For this reason alone, the best hope are those Soviet innovators who reason in terms of the existing system, whether they call themselves liberal socialists, communist reformers, democratic Marxist-Leninists, or simply doers of small deeds, and not those who repudiate the whole Soviet experience since 1917.

Second, much will depend upon the international environment, and thus American policy and behavior. Soviet reform has a chance only in conditions of a progressive relaxation of tensions between the USSR and its foreign adversaries. Worsening international relations will drive the Soviet Union back into her isolation and past, strengthening reactionaries and further diminishing reformers of all stripes. Or to take a different example, a complete break between the Soviet Communist Party and the Euro-Communist parties of Italy, France, and Spain would be an unfortunate development. These European parties have been a source of some restraint and liberal influence on the Soviet leadership, and a break would only further reduce this kind of Western influence and strengthen hard-line tendencies in the Soviet Union.

If this perspective on the future is one of guarded optimism, my last general point about the Soviet domestic scene is different. Despite the diversity of Soviet opinion, the predominant outlook, again both among officials and ordinary citizens, is a profound conservatism. This conservatism is strongest, of course, among the older generation, which still dominates middle and upper levels of officialdom, but it also appears to play a role in the attitudes of the younger generations.

By "Soviet conservatism" I mean the everyday gut sentiments that characterize social and political conservatism elsewhere, including in our own country. It is a deep sentimentality about one's own past, about the commonplace and familiar, an instinctive preference for existing routines and orthodoxies (however obsolete), and a fear of things new as somehow threatening and potentially chaotic. Politically, it is not always a flat rejection of any change; but it is an almost prohibitive insistence that change be very slow, tightly controlled, based on "law and order" (which is also a Soviet catchphrase) lest "things will be worse," and hence it is an instinctive, though often conditional, deference to political authorities that guard the present against the future, including the armed forces and the police.

That a system born in revolution and still professing revolutionary ideas should have become one of the most conservative in the world may seem preposterous. But history has witnessed other such transformations, as well as the frequent deradicalization of revolutionary ideologies.[5] Moreover, there are specific, and mutually reinforcing, sources of this Soviet conservatism. All of those factors variously said to be the most important in Soviet politics have contributed to it: the bureaucratic tradition of Russian government before the revolution; the subsequent bureaucratization of Soviet life, which proliferated conservative norms and created an entrenched class of zealous defenders of bureaucratic status and privilege; the geriatric nature of the present-day elite; and even the official ideology, whose thrust turned many years ago from the creation of a new social order to extolling the existing one.

Underlying all the factors making for Soviet conservatism is the Soviet historical experience, which is still for a great many citizens the story of their own lives. If few nations have achieved so much in so short a time, none has suffered such a traumatic history. In sixty years, man-made catastrophes have repeatedly victimized millions of Soviet citizens — the first European war, revolution, civil war, two great famines, forcible collectivization, Stalin's great terror, World War Two. Every family has lost someone dear, often more than once. These memories live with an intensity that is hard for us to imagine. The victims have often been the essential elite of any nation's progress — the young, the strong, the enterprising, the gifted. No less remarkable than the Soviet Union's achievements is the fact that they were accomplished in the face of these colossal losses. Out of this experience in living memory have developed the underlying joint pillars of Soviet conservatism—a sense of great national pride and earned prestige from the achievements, together with an anxiety that the next disaster forever looms and must be guarded against.

Because we are slow to recognize this conservatism, we have yet to calculate fully its influence either Soviet domestic or foreign politics. At home, it is an important bond — a truly collective sentiment — between the government and the majority of the people. It affects all areas of policymaking, all segments of the population, high and low, and even political dissidents, who fear internal turmoil as much as they object to the government.

Its influence on foreign policy cannot be easily exaggerated. Above all, this conservatism informs Soviet leaders' acute sense of national prestige, a crucial element in their outlook obscured by our rival notions that they are either aggressive ideologues or cynical realists. When offended, this prestige factor can cause them to postpone, or even jettison, international relations that they otherwise desire, be it economic, trade or arms limitation agreements. On the other hand, when they perceive a ratification of Soviet prestige and status, it can lead them to join in international agreements that included provisions not to their liking, such as the Helsinki accords of 1975.

To put this differently, we usually discuss Soviet policy in military terms of "strategic parity." This is important, of course. But the larger Soviet striving in recent times has been for political parity, equal respect as the other super-power — full recognition of its achievements and rightful place in the world. As with the United States, this striving means both conserving and where possible enhancing the Soviet Union's status in a changing world. It is manifest in the Soviet infatuation with traditional diplomatic protocol, global meddling, and obsessive counting of everything from Olympic medals to strategic weapons. And nothing is more insulting than persistent suggestions in the West that the achievements and power status of the Soviet Union are somehow illegitimate.

Righteous indignation about foreign "interference in our internal affairs" is often a hypocritical dodge. But when a Soviet official complains, to take a recent example, that "James Carter has assumed the role of mentor to the USSR,"[6] we hear the voice of hurt pride and genuine resentment. The "surprising adverse reaction in the Soviet Union to our stand on human rights," which President Carter now acknowledges, should have surprised no one. It proved to be "a greater obstacle to other friendly pursuits, common goals, like in SALT, than [President Carter] had anticipated"[7] because, contrary to American spokesmen, there was for Soviet leaders a "linkage." Perceiving a direct affront to their self-esteem, they reacted — as they did when confronted by the Jackson-Vanik and Stevenson Amendments in 1974 — accordingly, and predictably.

The ways that this conservatism can influence Soviet behavior are too numerous to explore here. A last example must suffice. American critics of detente and SALT see aggressive military intentions in the circumstance that "Americans think in terms of deterring war almost exclusively. The Soviet leaders think much more of what might happen in such a war."[8] Given the Soviet unpreparedness and loss of perhaps 20 million people in the last war, we should be surprised if it were otherwise. Indeed, a Soviet government that did not make some efforts in this direction, for example the civilian defense programs in which our anti-detente lobby sees such ominous implications, would hardly be a Soviet government at all.

## No Alternative to Detente

What does all this tell us more concretely about Soviet foreign policy and prescribe for American policy? For me there is no sane or moral or otherwise desirable alternative to what is now called, somewhat loosely, detente. If we begin with the simplest literal meaning of the word — a relaxation of historical tensions between Washington and Moscow — and with its foremost objective — a reduction of the possibilities of war through strategic arms control — the alternative, an "Era II of the Cold War," is plainly unacceptable in the nuclear age. Those Americans, and their Soviet counterparts, who insist that detente is a "one-way street," that "we have nothing to gain from it," or that the two countries share no basic interests, should say openly that they prefer a world of escalating arms races, nuclear proliferation, and mounting risks of mutual destruction by design or mishap.

Reducing the risks of nuclear war is the first, indispensable, and irreproachable reason for detente. There is, however, even among its American (and Soviet) advocates, a spectrum of thinking about the desirable nature and scope of detente. Some advocate a narrow policy centered almost exclusively on military issues. While this position is preferable to the flatly anti-detente one, it is one-dimensional and unrealistic. Cooperation in the area of military safeguards is inseparable from broader forms of cooperation that promote stable relations between the two countries. I favor a policy of detente that can go beyond relaxation of tensions to full relations on all levels, but one consistent with intractable realities and free of extravagant expectations. For this we need an understanding of detente considerably broader than today's events.

Just as the history of the cold war did not begin in 1947-48, but in 1917, what we now call detente did not begin in 1972. Leaving aside early milestones such as our belated recognition of the Soviet Union in 1933, the contemporary history of detente began in the Eisenhower-Khrushchev era, and not with the Nixon-Brezhnev phase. In short, detente is a historical process with previous stages of development that include both progress and setbacks. At different stages, quite different issues have been in the forefront and have defined the status of detente at the time — pullbacks from military confrontation, cultural exchanges, summitry, Berlin, Cuba, the Middle East, arms talks, trade, Jewish emigration, human rights.

It is therefore essential that detente as an ongoing and future process not be understood as something ultimately determined by one or more current events. This kind of political gimmickry, practiced sometimes by the opponents of detente as well as Nixon-Kissinger proponents of detente, can only produce unrealistic expectations and needless disillusionment, as we are now witnessing. A durable detente policy must be both historical and long-sighted.

Even in the best circumstances, there will be tough bargaining, resentment, serious misunderstandings, sharp disagreements, and open conflicts of national interests between the United States and the USSR. The goal is to reduce these elements progressively at each stage. We are, after all, talking about "detente" between long-standing rivals with very different social systems, political traditions, and orthodoxies, and not about Anglo-American relations. To imagine that these differences will disappear, or even diminish notably, in an appointed time because of proclamations is dangerous nonsense.[9] To promise detente without conflict, or to reject detente because of the conflict, is silly illogic. It is like saying that the job of diplomacy is only to formalize what already unites nations, and not to reconcile what divides them.

Two primary conditions for a progressively broadening detente are already present. First, there are substantial domestic forces for detente in both countries, despite parallel controversies about its dangers, strong opposition, and fluctuating internal conditions. Alarmist warnings about secret Soviet "intentions" and strategic "blueprints" fly in the face of the realities. Escalating military expenditures, the danger of mutual destruction, economic problems, and other domestic factors have brought a sizable part even of the conservative Soviet establishment away from old autarchic habits to acceptance of fuller relations with the West.

In other words, the main thrust of Soviet conservatism today is to preserve what it already has at home and abroad, not to jeopardize it. A conservative government is, of course, capable of dangerous militaristic actions, as we saw in Czechoslovakia and Vietnam; but these are acts of imperial protectionism, a kind of defensive militarism, not a revolutionary or aggrandizing one. It is certainly true that for most Soviet leaders, as presumably for most American leaders, detente is not an altruistic endeavor but the pursuit of national interests. In one sense, this is sad. But it is probably also true that mutual self-interest provides a more durable basis for detente than lofty, and finally empty, altruism.

The second existing condition is a shared philosophy of detente. Both sides now officially define detente as including both cooperation and competition, in peaceful conditions, between the two countries. If cooperation through SALT eliminates or significantly reduces military competition, we have no reason to fear the other kinds of competition, assuming we have confidence in our system. If American business firms cannot be allowed to trade freely with Soviet agencies, it speaks poorly for the capitalism the United States claims to profess. If the Soviet leadership's refusal to give up what it calls "ideological struggle," which so alarms our critics of detente, deters us, this speaks poorly for our own ideology, which emphasizes the virtue of conflicting ideas.

Without exaggerating or blinking away the competitive and conflictual aspects, we should pursue the cooperative component of detente vigorously and imaginatively. Global areas of cooperation, such as strategic arms control, ecology, and food shortages, may require protracted negotiations and the participation of other nations. But there is a wide range of immediate opportunities for fuller bilateral relations in the areas of trade, education, culture, science, sports, and tourism, to name a few.

Detente is too important to be left to governments alone. A variety of nongovernmental American organizations and citizens have been pursuing these kinds of relations, sometimes in the face of official American indifference and even obstructionism, for many years. They should be encouraged, and their ideas and expertise solicited, so that detente will become not merely fuller government-to-government relations, but institution-to-institution, profession-to-profession, citizen-to-citizen relations, both as a buffer against leadership changes in both countries and as a way of building popular support here and in the Soviet Union. Meanwhile, the American government should make its own direct contribution by, among other things, promoting trade by granting to the Soviet Union favorable tariff and credit provisions,[10] funding larger and more diverse exchanges of people, and pressing for liberalized entry-visa procedures and fewer travel restrictions in both countries.

American policy alone cannot, of course, guarantee the future of detente. This requires no less a pro-detente Soviet leadership with sufficient support in its own high establishment to withstand the inevitable setbacks in Soviet-American relations. And this returns us to the Soviet domestic scene.

Supporters of the Jackson-Vanik Amendment and other restrictions on detente have, so to speak, a half-idea. They argue, correctly, that the future of detente must be related to change inside the Soviet Union. Unfortunately, they seem not to understand that domestic change can also be for the worse, and that liberalizing change depends upon the respective political fortunes of trends and groups inside the Soviet establishment. These proponents of a kind of remote American interventionism in Soviet politics violate what should be our first axiom: We do not have the wisdom or the power, or the right, to try directly to shape change inside the Soviet Union.[11] Any foreign government that becomes deeply involved in Soviet internal politics, or for that matter in Soviet emigre politics (whose many different "ambassadors" will continue to appeal to us), will do itself and others more harm than good.

What the United States can and should do is influence Soviet liberalization *indirectly* by developing a long-term American foreign policy, and thereby an international environment, that will strengthen reformist trends and undermine reactionary ones inside the Soviet Union. This means a further relaxation of tensions, increasing contacts on all levels, and drawing the Soviet Union into full, stable, relations with the Western countries — in short, detente. This is not, in the lingering rhetoric of another generation, "appeasement." Such a policy allows for hard bargaining for our own national interests and private demands for certain kinds of Soviet behavior. But it is predicated on an American conduct that takes into account the nature of Soviet conservatism and is not calculated to offend needlessly the self-image and prestige of the Soviet establishment. Our new interventionists fail on all counts. Bombastic ultimatums, discriminatory congressional restrictions, and condescending preachments addressed publicly to the Soviet leadership offend the conservative majority, vivify the xenophobic prophecies of the reactionaries, and make meaningful reform suspect, if not impossible, as a concession to outside pressure.

## The "Human Rights" Campaign

This brings us, finally, to the issue of political rights* in the Soviet Union, which (for better or worse) has become a central focus in our current debate over detente. The question is terribly complex, even agonizing, especially for people with first-hand knowledge of the Soviet Union. And like other issues that are translated superficially into a Manichean choice between morality and immorality, it creates acrimonious divisions and false illusions.

Our own disagreements about American policy toward Soviet political rights should be among Americans equally committed to political liberties as a universal principle. The real question is not the validity of this princi-

---

*The Carter Administration has defined this issue in terms of Soviet "human rights," which is inexact. The issue is political rights or liberties. The term "human rights" includes a whole range of economic and other welfare problems, in which the Soviet Union, in the world context, can boast considerable achievement.

ple, but whether specific American policies actually promote political liberties and safeguard dissent in the Soviet Union. There are, for example, knowledgeable Westerners who have had extensive contact with Soviet dissidents over the years, who admire them as courageous individuals and as representatives of a noble cause, but who have deep misgivings about recent American measures in this area. Furthermore, speaking for myself, it is fully consistent to want a larger moral aspect in American foreign policy, especially after our immoral and even criminal commissions in Vietnam and Chile, and still disapprove of certain American measures directed against Soviet violations of political rights. This does not reflect, as is sometimes charged, a bias in favor of left-wing dictatorships and against right-wing ones, but concern for the actual consequences of a specific policy.

American proponents of a hard-line policy exhort us to rally behind "our friends, the Soviet dissidents." But the Soviet dissident community is itself deeply divided into at least three groups on the question of American policy.[12] The larger group does insist that a tough American line on behalf of Soviet political rights has been, and will continue to be, only beneficial. They want more, and stronger, of the same. A second group acknowledges that recent American actions have caused the democratic movement setbacks and hardships, but insists that they will be beneficial in the long-run — how and when is left unclear. The third group argues that tougher American policies, from Senator Jackson's to President Carter's, have had, and can only have, a negative impact because, by going beyond diplomatic pressure to open confrontation, they galvanize Soviet conservative and reactionary opposition and jeopardize both active dissidents and reformers inside the Soviet system.

General references to "the Soviet dissidents" are therefore meaningless. Dissident opinion is far too diverse. Indeed, there are even Orthodox nationalist dissidents who dislike both detente and American interference in Soviet affairs. But even the numerical fact that most dissident activists want a hard-line American policy does not prove its wisdom. It reflects instead the fact that since 1972 many Soviet protesters have increasingly lost hope in internal sources of change and thus, for reasons of politics and morale, have looked increasingly to pressure from outside and specifically from the United States. We can understand this psychological development; but good sense tells us that it is bad for us and for them.

The proof is, as we say, in the pudding. President Carter's human rights campaign of early 1977 (insofar as it was directed at the Soviet Union), like earlier measures linking trade and detente to levels of Jewish emigration, has done more harm than good. It may be inexact to call President Carter's campaign a policy since, as Andrew Young has stated, it "was never really set down, thought out and planned."[13] It may even be that the campaign originated as much with domestic American political concerns.

Whatever the case, the "adverse reaction in the Soviet Union" was unanticipated. Though it is possible that a new Soviet crackdown on dissidents was planned even before President Carter took office, the nature and dimensions of the crackdown were made worse by American statements and actions. Each dramatic act of the Carter Administration's campaign — sharp warnings on behalf of Soviet dissidents in late January, the President's personal letter to Andrei Sakharov in early February, his White House meeting with exiled dissident Vladimir Bukovsky in early March — was followed by new acts of Soviet repression at home, from the arrests of Aleksandr Ginzburg and Yuri Orlov in February to the interrogation of American correspondent Robert Toth in June. We must see clearly what ensued — a dangerous game of political chicken, reminiscent of the cold war, played at the highest levels. ("We're not going to back down," declared President Carter.)[14] The victims were both our "common goals" and Soviet dissidents themselves.

Why did the Carter Administration's campaign become counterproductive? I do not think that the reason is to be found in the President's general statements on human rights and Helsinki. In signing these accords, the Soviet leadership must have reconciled itself to something along these lines, particularly from a new American administration, as part of the "ideological struggle." The reason was rather the way in which the campaign directly assaulted, even if only inadvertently, all those aspects of Soviet conservatism I discussed earlier. Two highly publicized episodes — the President's letter to Sakharov and the White House invitation to Bukovsky — are vivid examples.

The Carter campaign began in January, 1977, and thus coincided with the sixtieth anniversary year of the Russian revolution, when Soviet conservatism and official self-esteem are in continuous celebration and at their most acute. The Administration's first statements and President Carter's letter then came on the heels of an extraordinary event and one of Sakharov's rare mistakes — his public suggestion that Soviet authorities themselves were responsible for the fatal bombing in a Moscow subway in early January. Scarcely any dissidents took this suggestion seriously, and Sakharov himself later seemed to regret it.[15] More important, the bombing was an exceptional event that greatly alarmed and embarrassed Soviet authorities. The decision to issue a Presidential statement on Soviet civil rights in the form of a letter to Sakharov on this unusual occasion was, to be kind, very bad judgment. Nothing could have been more offensive to official Soviet sensibilities or to have assured a stronger reaction. (It may also have confirmed doubts among some Soviet officials about the authenticity of American concern for Soviet political rights.)

The Bukovsky affair raises similar questions of judgment. In December 1976, the Soviet government exchanged Bukovsky, a defiant and brave dissident then in his eleventh year of prison camps and mental hospitals, for the jailed Chilean Communist leader Luis Corvalan. This, too, was an extraordinary development. The Soviet Union not only dealt equally with what it calls a "fascist dictatorship," it also acknowledged for the first time its own political prisoners. International publicity had made Bukovsky's personal fate an embarrassment. But it seems likely that the Soviet decision to risk its prestige in this dramatic way also had the larger purpose of weighing the feasibility, and political costs, of future agreements for the release of other Soviet prisoners.

Any such possibility was aborted, at least for the time, by President Carter's invitation to Bukovsky. Their meeting, which had the earmarks of a public relations coup against former President Ford's rebuff to Aleksandr Solzhenitsyn, allowed Bukovsky to denounce the Soviet government from the White House, implied that his release was a triumph of American policy, and thereby probably persuaded Soviet leaders that the political costs of such releases were too high. If our real concern is the plight of people, and not a propaganda victory, where is the morality in this outcome?

The same criticism applies to earlier American campaigns, culminating in the Jackson-Vanik Amendment of 1974, to make trade and detente dependent upon levels of Soviet Jewish emigration. The net effect was, as we know, to diminish that emigration considerably. But other questions were similarly ignored during the presidential primary season, when the issue of Jewish emigration came to the fore. Did the almost exclusive focus on Jews who wished to leave, with scant regard for other groups, reflect a moral commitment to the principle of open borders or the political power of Jewish lobbies in this country? How much thought was given to the frightful backlash that this campaign was certain to have on Soviet Jews who did not wish to emigrate? And how can monthly or annual quotas, and Soviet compliance, be determined when no one knows how many Jews actually want to leave?

The case against these kinds of short-sighted, highly publicized, and politically volatile campaigns that link American policy to specific events, issues, or prominent dissidents inside the Soviet Union is, I think, overwhelming. They involve us in complexities and ramifications beyond our control and in moral ambiguities beyond our resolution. Inside the United States, they encourage a revival of cold-war attitudes which could again distort our own domestic priorities, while undermining public support for detente. Internationally, they generate tensions and confrontations between Moscow and Washington detrimental to our mutual interests, endanger private concessions already granted by Soviet and East European authorities (in the area of family reunification, for example),[16] and, perhaps most important, they create an atmosphere unconducive to Soviet liberalization. Inside the Soviet Union, they arouse the conservative majority against American "interference," taint both dissidents and reformers as "Western agents," abet the party's neo-Stalinist wing, and further divide and misguide the dissident community.[17]

Indeed, the most ominous of recent Soviet reactions is neither the new arrests, which arguably would have come anyway, nor the setbacks in SALT negotiations, which after a decent interlude will move ahead, but the official Soviet campaign linking dissidents, and potentially any reformer, to the American government and specifically to the CIA. The emptiness of this charge is matched only by its grim revival of one of the worst themes of the Stalinist past. It seems to be, alas, a response to the Carter Administration's own campaign and plain evidence that the neo-Stalinists have gained new influence in Soviet affairs.[18]

## The Lessons To Be Learned

The lessons to be learned are not all negative. They teach us that whatever potential the American government has for influence on the Soviet leadership in the area of political rights must be exercised in private negotiations and not through public ultimatums, sermons, and other confrontations of national prestige. Since "quiet diplomacy" appears to have acquired a sinister connotation, let us call it simply "diplomacy."

The Soviet leadership wants detente and the various agreements that it encompasses. In the proper place and manner, American representatives, from the President to State Department officials, can and should make clear that American public support for these relations depends significantly upon the status of political rights in the Soviet Union. Modest concessions and achievements are possible, certainly at first in the areas of emigration and family reunification. Despite its abominations in other areas, the Nixon-Kissinger administration did in fact achieve a great deal in this way. If our purpose is to help people, why scorn it?

At the same time, the American government should push for fuller relations at all levels with the Soviet Union. Not only because this will promote a general international environment more conducive to Soviet liberalization, but because these diverse contacts create additional opportunities for direct influence. The Soviet Union has demonstrated its desire for expanded, regularized transactions with, for example, American business, scientific, and other academic groups, which in turn gives these groups some influence on their Soviet counterparts and thus indirectly on Soviet policy-makers.

Moreover, it is at this profession-to-profession level that outcries against specific violations of political rights can be most effective. A good example is the campaign on behalf of Academician Sakharov waged successfully by the American Academy of Sciences in 1973. An organized protest by a professional association and directed to its Soviet counterpart is more effective because it does not directly confront the Soviet government's prestige, it allows the Soviet leadership at least the fiction of referring the matter to a lesser Soviet body, and it thus draws a broader (and frequently more liberal) segment of Soviet officialdom into the deliberations. In brief, unlike official campaigns by the American President or Congress, it leaves room for concessions.

The final guideline simply reiterates the axiom I tried to formulate earlier. Any policies that involve the American government deeply in the quite different world of Soviet domestic (or emigre) politics will end badly. It is neither indifferent nor platitudinous to emphasize that the Soviet future must be decided by people in the Soviet Union and in their own way. I believe that even modest reform within the existing system would be good for them, for us, and for the world, and that this remains a real possibility. But the main contribution our government can make is more concern for our own problems at home, and a calm policy of restraint and detente abroad.

# Notes

[1] See, for example, A. Katsenelinboigen, "Coloured Markets in the Soviet Union," *Soviet Studies,* January, 1977, pp. 62-85.

[2] As an example of how these problems are related and create interlocking constraints, consider the following. Beginning with the Khrushchev period, the Soviet leadership has made repeated promises, and unfolded several unsuccessful campaigns, to satisfy the consumer desires of the population. This is, I think, a genuine commitment, deriving partly from ideological tenets of communism, which sounds in official statements increasingly like the Welfare State plus consumerism, and partly from a need to counter political demands of the intelligentsia. But this commitment to a mass consumer-goods program is inseparable from other areas of domestic and foreign policy. It involves a restructuring of economic life and thus raises the question of reforms in the planning, industrial, and agricultural sectors. It involves new techniques of economic decision making and thus the problem of centralized power. It involves capital investments and allocations incompatible with escalating military budgets and grandiose commitments abroad. Meanwhile, Soviet consumerism is part of the leadership's concept of a peaceful competition abroad with the United States, as well as its anxiety that working-class discontents over prices and wages in Eastern Europe could be replicated in the Soviet Union.

[3] Ilya Erenburg, the late Soviet writer, once remarked, complaining about some of his fellow party members, that the problem with having only one party is that anybody can get in.

[4] There are several informed accounts of these trends, though categories and labels sometimes vary. See, for example, Roy A. Medvedev, *On Socialist Democracy* (New York, 1975), chap. iii: and Alexander Yanov, *Detente After Brezhnev: The Domestic Roots of Soviet Foreign Policy* (Berkeley, California, 1977). Much first-hand information on reformers and neo-Stalinists is available in the *samizdat* journal *Politicheskii dnevnik* (2 vols; Amsterdam, 1972 and 1975). Since the 1950's, these trends have been associated with, and articulated in, various official journals.

[5] See Robert C. Tucker, *The Marxian Revolutionary Idea* (New York, 1969), chap. vi.

[6] *The New York Times,* June 9, 1977.

[7]*Ibid.,* June 26, 1977.

[8]Paul Nitze quoted in Charles Gati and Toby Trister Gati, *The Debate Over Detente* (Headline Series, No. 234; New York, 1977) p. 27.

[9]Historians will find some whimsy, or at least understatement, in the following: "Two years is a relatively short time in which to alter the long-standing practices of sovereign nations, either in regard to one another or to their citizenries." The Commission on Security and Cooperation in Europe, *Report to the Congress of the United States on Implementation of the Final Act of the Conference on Security and Cooperation in Europe: Findings and Recommendations Two Years After Helsinki* (Washington, August 1, 1977), p. 5.

[10]This means, of course, reviving the Trade Act of 1972 by repealing the Jackson-Vanik Amendment and the Stevenson Amendment, which severely restricted Export-Import Bank credits to the USSR. For a persuasive argument in favor of expanding trade, see Daniel Yergin, "Politics and Soviet-American Trade: The Three Questions," *Foreign Affairs,* April, 1977, pp. 517-38; and on the more general aspects of detente, Marshall D. Shulman, "On Learning to Live With Authoritarian Regimes," *ibid.,* January, 1977, pp. 325-38.

[11]An unfortunate example of this lack of wisdom and potential for mischief was Senator Jackson's attack on the well-known dissident Roy Medvedev as "nothing but a front man, a sycophant for the leadership." Senator Jackson went on to liken Medvedev to "certain Jews [who] fronted for Goering, Goebbels, and Hitler." *The New York Times,* January 28, 1975. Expelled from the party, subjected to periodic searches, and out-of-work, Medvedev is a democratic Marxist who tries to speak to and for reformers inside the party.

[12]For a full examination of this subject, see Frederick C. Barghoorn, *Detente and the Democratic Movement in the USSR* (New York, 1976).

[13]*The Washington Post,* June 6, 1977.

[14]*The New York Times,* January 31, 1977.

[15]Various explanations of the bombing circulated in Moscow. The most frequent theory linked it to food shortages, poor living conditions, rumors of price increases, and other discriminatory practices in provincial towns outside Moscow. This theory viewed it as a Polish-style protest.

[16]Prime Minister Trudeau and Chancellor Schmidt have expressed concern, for example, that increased movement of people from Eastern Europe to Canada and West Germany may be jeopardized. *The New York Times,* July 17, 1977. Austrian Chancellor Kreisky expressed similar concerns earlier. *The International Herald Tribune,* March 16, 1977.

[17]On February 7, 1977, the prominent dissident Yuri Orlov said publicly, "I think after the State Department statement on Ginzburg I will not be arrested." He was arrested three days later. This is, of course, subject to different interpretations, one being that Orlov's own statement made certain his arrest.

[18]On March 21, 1977, in a speech little noted outside the Soviet Union, Brezhnev made an unusual distinction between internal critics. Constructive critics were to be thanked; mistaken but "honest" critics were to be forgiven; but "anti-Soviet" critics, who had Western support and were often "imperialist agents," were to be punished. In the Soviet context, these distinctions suggested some flexibility and even a little "liberalism." My guess is that Brezhnev was trying to guard against neo-Stalinist excesses in the anti-dissident campaign. See *Komsomol'skaia Pravda,* March 22, 1977.

48458

# NEEDED: A NEW AMERICAN VIEW OF THE USSR
## By George F. Kennan

J ust 60 years ago there came into being the present political regime in
Russia. And exactly at the halfway point of that span of time — 30
years ago — I chanced to deliver a talk on the subject of Soviet-American
relations which became the basis for an article in the magazine Foreign
Affairs signed by the pseudonym "X." This article attained a certain
melancholy notoriety and has dogged my footsteps ever since, like a
faithful, but unwanted and somewhat embarrassing animal.

The coincidence of chronology naturally leads me to reflect on the
changes that have occurred since that year of 1947 in the background
against which Soviet-American relations have had to proceed. The Russian political scene was then dominated by a single great personality — a
man whom Churchill very aptly called a "crafty giant" — a man of enormous political-tactical genius — a formidable opponent on anyone's
terms, but one whose combination of paranoia with cruelty and political
mastery had served to create one of the great totalitarian monstrosities of
our time: a personal depotism as ruthless and far-reaching as anything the
modern world has ever known. By 1947 this depotism had already cost
the Soviet peoples several millions of lives. And it had not stopped at the
old Russian borders but had been extended — and this with our tacit
blessing — to nearly one-half of the remainder of the European continent.
And no one could be sure, in 1947, that it would stop there.

The danger was not one of further military conquest. (Actually, it never
has been that.) The problem was that Western Europe, still dazed, shaken
and jittery from the effects of the Hitlerian conquest, did not know what
to expect. Its peoples lacked confidence in themselves. They had a
tendency to rush for safety to the side of whoever they thought was likely

George Kennan, former Ambassador to Moscow and
currently at the Institute for Advanced Studies in Princeton,
is the senior American expert on the Soviet Union. His ideas
here were first presented to a Washington meeting of the
Council on Foreign Relations and then published in the
Washington Post on Dec. 11, 1977.

to win in the end. They would have been quite capable of throwing themselves into the arms of their own Communist parties if they gained the impression that those Communist parties represented the wave of the future. And to this had to be added the fact that the Moscow center, and Stalin personally, enjoyed at that time a total monopolistic control over the world Communist movement — a control which meant that any success by any Communist party anywhere in seizing power within its own country had to be regarded as equivalent in its effects to a military conquest by the Soviet Union.

## Moderate Soviet Leadership

It is enough to cite these circumstances, I think, to make clear the magnitude of the changes that have occurred in this 30-year interval. The Soviet Union remains, of course, an authoritarian state — much as was the pre-revolutionary Tsarist Russia; but there is very little to be seen today of the terror that prevailed in Stalin's time; and the regime is headed by a moderate, in fact conservative man; a man who, whatever other failings of outlook he may have, is a man of the middle, a skilled balancer among political forces — a man confidently regarded by all who know him as a man of peace.

Moscow's monopoly of authority over the world Communist movement has been thoroughly disrupted — so much so that even in the case of those Communist parties that still ostensibly recognize the Soviet leadership, the lines of authority leading from Moscow are tenuous and incapable of bearing much weight. It is a case where the semblance of authority can be retained only by the sacrifice of much of the reality.

And finally, in place of the anxious, jittery Western Europe of 1947 we now have an area which is unquestionably the seat of some of the most successful civilization, economically and socially, that the modern world has to show. The change, to be sure, has not been complete. People have not fully overcome the trauma of two world wars. Many still lack confidence in themselves, see dangers on every hand, require to be reassured periodically, like frightened children. This situation has its military implications, and plays a part, of course, in Soviet-American relations. But it cannot be compared in seriousness and dangerousness to the situation we faced in 1947.

Now all these changes, and others I might cite, have run in the direction of an improvement in the objective possibilities for a better Soviet-American relationship. This does not mean, of course, possibilities for a complete normalization of those relations. For that there remain too many obstacles — historical, psychological and ideological. There has always been, and remains today, an area in which no complete political intimacy is possible, where interests must remain competitive and in part conflicting.

But there is also another area, an area in which interests largely coincide and limited collaboration is possible. In the light of the changes we have just had occasion to note, this latter area has tended, slowly but steadily, to grow. And where sensible efforts have been put forward on both sides to take advantage of this situation — where people have tried, in other words, to create a balanced, businesslike and realistic relationship between two very disparate political systems — the results, given patience and persistence, have not been discouraging.

This was true, among others, in the period of the Nixon-Kissinger detente. Progress was made in a number of fields which was more than negligible and from which both sides are continuing to benefit today. The fact that these achievements were somewhat overdramatized, that they led to unreal expectations and gave rise to some disillusionment when these expectations were not met, should not blind us to their positive residue.

Nevertheless, the effort to pursue a balanced and useful middle course in the relationship with Russia has never been an easy one for American policymakers to follow; and one of the main reasons why this has been so difficult is that seldom, if ever, have we had an adequate consensus in American opinion on the nature of the problem and the most promising ways of approaching it.

Prior to the late 1940s — prior, that is, to the Korean War and the death of Stalin — the difficulty seemed to come primarily from the left: from people who had a naive, overtrusting, overidealistic view of what was then Stalinist power — people who thought it really possible for this country to ingratiate itself with the Stalin regime by various one-sided gestures of confidence and generosity and reproached our government for not doing so. It was, incidentally, against this sort of left-wing deviation that the "X-article," and the policy of containment, were directed.

## The Anti-Soviet Opposition

But since Stalin's death, the opposition to an even-handed and realistic policy toward Russia has tended to come from the opposite end of the political spectrum: from people who were unable to see the curious mix of the negative and the positive, of the discouraging and the hopeful, in the Soviet political personality — people who could see only the negative, and who feared the consequences of anything less than a total rejection and hostility from our side.

There has never been a time in these last 25 years, it seems to me, when this opposition has not made itself felt. There has never been a time when American statesmen concerned to find and develop a constructive middle-ground in relations with Russia have not felt their efforts harassed from this direction.

And the harrassment has not been minor in intensity or in power. Every administration has been to some extent afraid of this hard-line opposition.

It had behind it the power of chauvinist rhetoric as well as that of strict military logic. It had the capability of hurling at any and all opponents the charge of being "soft on communism;" and however meaningless this phrase may be, it is a formidable weapon in a society unhappily vulnerable to the power of the slogan.

In the heyday of the Nixon-Kissinger detente, this opposition was almost silenced — partly by Richard Nixon's formidable credentials as a hard-liner, which bewildered many critics, and partly by Henry Kissinger's diplomatic fireworks, which dazzled them. But the resulting silence was one of frustration, not of acceptance. When Watergate drained the authority of this political combination, the opposition broke forth once again with redoubled strength and violence. It has raged over the entire period from 1975 to the present. It sufficed to knock out the 1972 trade agreement and to lower the level of Soviet-American trade. It sufficed to delay the approach to a new SALT agreement. And it has achieved today, against the background of a new administration and a somewhat unstructured Congress, a power it never had before. It now claims to have — and, for all I know, it does have — the power to veto any Soviet-American agreements in the military or the economic field that do not meet with its requirements; and such are its requirements that I come increasingly to suspect that this means, in effect, any conceivable agreements at all.

I have made my best efforts to understand the rationale of this opposition. Many of the bearers of it are my friends. I know them as honorable people. I do not suspect, or disrespect, their motives.

It is clear that we have to do here with a complex phenomenon, not a simple one. This body of opinion embraces some people whose trouble seems to be that they are unaware of the changes between 1947 and 1977, who talk of the problems of Soviet-American relations in terms of identical with those used at the height of the Cold War — who sometimes seem, in fact, unaware that Stalin is dead.

Then, there are others whose emotions have been aroused over the question of human rights, of Jewish emigration, and who would like to see American policy directed not to an accommodation to Soviet power as it is but to the changing of the very nature of the Soviet regime.

## Military Myopia

More important, however, than either of these are the people who view the relationship exclusively as one of military rivalry — who see in it no significant values or issues or possibilities other than ones relating to the supposed determination of the Soviet leadership to achieve some sort of decisive military ascendancy over the NATO coalition — and this, of course, with the most menacing and deadly of intent. These include outstandingly the military planners, whose professional obligation it is to set up a planner's dummy of any possible military opponent, to endow that dummy with just the motivation I have described, and then to treat it as if it were real. But this group also includes many non-military people who, accepting this dummy as the reality, lose themselves in the fantastic reaches of what I might call military mathematics — the mathematics of possible mutual destruction in an age of explosively burgeoning weapons technology.

Like many of the rest of you, I have made my efforts to understand the arguments of these military enthusiasts. I have tried to follow them through the mazes of their intricate and sophisticated calculations of possible military advantage at various future points in time. I have tried to follow them in their recital of the letters and numbers of various weapons systems, some real, some imagined, their comparisons of the reputed capacities of these systems, their computations of the interactions of them in situations of actual hostility.

I come away from this exercise frustrated, and with two overpowering impressions. The first is that this entire science of long-range massive destruction — of calculated advantage or disadvantage in modern weaponry — has gotten seriously out of hand; that the variables, the complexities, the uncertainties it involves are rapidly growing beyond the power of either human mind or computer.

But my second impression is that there is a distinct unreality about this whole science of destruction — unreality, that is, when you view it as the plane on which our differences over policy have to be resolved. I doubt that we are going to solve our problems by trying to agree as to whether the Russians will or will not have the capability of "taking out" our land-based missiles at some time in the 1980s. I doubt that this is the heart of the problem. I suspect that something deeper is involved. And if I had to try to define that deeper something, I would have to say that it is the view one takes of the nature of the Soviet leadership and of the discipline exerted upon it by its own experiences, problems and political necessities.

## Two Views of Soviet Leadership

There are basically two views of this leadership: two ways in which it is seen in this country. In one of these views, the Soviet leaders appear as a terrible and forbidding group of men — monsters of sorts, really, because lacking in all elements of common humanity — men totally dedicated either to the destruction or to the political undoing and enslavement of this country and its allies — men who have all internal problems, whether of civic obedience or of economic development, essentially solved and are therefore free to spend their time evolving elaborate schemes for some ultimate military showdown — men who are prepared to accept the most tremendous risks, and to place upon their people the most fearful sacrifices, if only in this way their program of destruction or domination of ourselves and our allies can be successfully carried forward.

That is one view. In the other view, these leaders are seen as a group of quite ordinary men, to some extent the victims, if you will, of the ideology on which they have been reared, but shaped far more importantly by the discipline of the responsibilities they and their predecessors have borne as rulers of a great country in the modern technological age. They are seen, in this view, as highly conservative men, perhaps the most conservative ruling group to be found anywhere in the world, markedly advanced in age, approaching the end of their tenure and given to everything else but rash adventure. They are seen as men who share the horror of major war that dominates most of the Soviet people, who have no desire to experience another military conflagration and no intention to launch one — men more seriously concerned to preserve the present limits of their political power and responsibility than to expand those limits — men whose motivation is essentially defensive and whose attention is riveted primarily to the unsolved problems of economic development within their own country. They are seen as men who suffer greatly under the financial burden which the maintenance of the present bloated arsenals imposes on the Soviet economy, and who would like to be relieved of that burden if this could be accomplished without undue damage to Russia's security and to their own political prestige. They are seen, finally, as men who are, to be sure, seldom easy to deal with, who care more about appearances than about reality, who have an unfortunate fixation about secrecy which complicates their external relations in many ways, but who, despite all these handicaps, have good and sound reason, rooted in their own interests, for desiring a peaceful and constructive relationship with the United States within the area where that is theoretically possible.

It is these two conflicting views of the Soviet leadership that lie at the heart of the conflict between those in our government who are attempting to make progress in our relations with the Soviet Union and those who are attacking this effort from the right. And the burden of what I have to say is that I think we can no longer permit this great conflict of outlook and opinion to go on in so large degree unreconciled as it has gone in recent years — that the moment has come when we can no longer carry on safely or effectively in our relations with the Soviet Union without the creation of a much wider consensus of opinion behind our policies of the moment than anything we have known in this recent period.

## Soviet-American Relations
## At a Crucial Point

We stand at a crucial point in Soviet-American relations. The expiration of the 1972 SALT agreement has confronted us with fundamental decisions. Either we move forward, boldly, confidently and imaginatively, to the creation of a new relationship with that country in the military field, or we deliver up ourselves and the rest of the civilized world to the appalling dangers of a nuclear weapons race totally out of control — a development devoid of any visible hopeful end, devoid of any imaginable end at all other than a wholly disastrous and apocalyptic one.

But our ability to pursue the more hopeful of these alternatives is today seriously jeopardized by lack of the consensus to which I just referred. The opposition now being brought to bear against the efforts of the President and the Secretary of State to carry forward negotiations in the field of the limitation of armaments has reached a degree of intensity that seems to me to exceed anything we have known in the past. Powerful efforts are being made, the tendency of which is not to bring about the failure of ratification of instruments already negotiated (nobody could object to that as a matter of procedure) but to discredit the very process of negotiation, and this at a very early stage. People are being attacked not for what they are known to have done in the negotiating process but for what they are presumed capable of doing — presumed capable on the basis of rumor or of calculated leak. They are being attacked, in other words, not for their actions but for their supposed intentions.

I am not questioning the motivation for these attacks. I can conceive that it may be, in many instances, of the highest. But I find myself wondering whether effective negotiations can be conducted in the face of opposition of this nature, particularly when we, as well as our Soviet counterparts, are being assured daily that the people who carry forward this opposition have not only the political power to torpedo any agreements or understanding that might realistically be arrived at, but also the firm intention to do so. Negotiating policy, it seems to me, cannot be effectively made or implemented against such a background.

And this present moment is one at which we simply cannot afford to have the force and momentum of our policy lamed in this manner. The stakes are too high. The penalties of failure are too serious. The implications of such a failure would carry even farther than just the prospect of an unlimited weapons race. A breakdown of the relationship on the military level could not fail to have — indeed, has already had to some extent — effects on other levels as well. And here, too, we have — and the world has — too much to lose to permit such a failure to occur.

We face in this coming period a tragically high probability of deepening crises in Southern Africa and in the Middle East. It may well be that the peace of the world will depend, as these crises develop, on the ability of the American and Soviet governments to remain in close communication, to give each other reasonable reassurance as to their intentions, and to coordinate their actions with a view to preventing local conflicts from growing to global dimensions.

Beyond this, we have the fact that these coming years are bound to see extensive changes in political leadership at the Soviet end. Nothing could be more unfortunate, surely, than that a new and inexperienced team of leaders should come into power in the Soviet Union confronting what would appear to be a blank wall of hostility and rejection at the American end — a situation in the face of which they would see no choice but to look for alternatives other than those of good relations with the United States. This is no time to foreclose other people's options, and particularly not the options of people new to the experience of power and obliged to define new lines of policy that may represent commitments for many years to come.

## Toward a Workable Consensus

These, then, are the reasons why it appears to me as an inescapable necessity that we should move promptly and resolutely to the achievement of a more workable consensus behind our policy towards the Soviet Union to take the place of the resounding disagreements that affect, and threaten to paralyze, the formulation and execution of policy in this field today.

I realize, of course, that it is easier to call attention to the need for such a consensus than to chart out the ways in which it could be achieved.

I realize, too, that behind a certain portion of this critical opinion there are commitments of an emotional or political or professional nature which are unlikely to be overcome by appeals to mere reason, and which will have to be confronted, as a political problem, by the responsible political leaders.

But in another portion of this spectrum we have to do with sincerely held and rational opinions, with conclusions drawn from what people believe to be the facts — from the spectrum of facts, or supposed facts, that they now have before them; and I wonder whether, in the case of these people in particular, approaches and devices could not be found — approaches and devices of a basically intellectual-nature which would help us importantly, and possibly even decisively, to get on with the solution of this problem. The problem is, after all, a cognitive one; and there is no reason why men of good will should not be able to come to some elements of agreement on the implications for policy of a given body of factual material if they can be brought to a common acceptance of its validity.

And here there are, as I see it, two requirements. First of all, I would propose that we lay aside completely, at least for the moment and for purpose of this exercise I have in mind, the whole question of the military relationship and all the arguments about who could conceivably do what to whom if their intentions were of the nastiest; and that we elevate our vision, at least for the time being, to the question of the real nature and situation of the particular foreign power we are dealing with.

And then, starting with that resolution, I can see in my mind's eye a series of private gatherings in which would be included not only high-level policy-makers of the moment but leading figures of this opposition, as well as possibly a few of others of us who are interested in Russian affairs — gatherings where we would come together not primarily to discuss matters among ourselves — not to air our prejudices and convictions on the basis of our present knowledge and our present ignorance, but where we would all listen humbly to what could be told to us by the most experienced and knowledgeable people who could be found in the respective fields — I avoid the word "expert" because it implies something more narrow than what I have in mind.

What I am thinking of, in other words, is a certain process of re-education in the realities of Soviet power and leadership — a common effort on the part of all of us who have been prominently involved in this debate — a process in which we would check our existing views at the door, together with our hats, and would listen and ask questions and try to get a new view of the facts before we drew conclusions. I suspect that in an experience of this nature, designed not to promote the clash of old views but to make possible the common development of new, more realistic and more up-to-date ones, we would come closer than in any other way to the composing of our differences.

And there is room for this, I assure you, because no more in the Soviet Union than anywhere else have things been standing still. There are available to us today masses of new factual material on conditions in the Soviet Union — material which, given the rather low state of Soviet studies in our country, has scarcely been digested by the scholars, much less by the policy-makers, the critics and the old-timers in this field of expertise. And in this latter category I include myself. I am much aware that it is exactly 50 years ago that I entered on my own career as a so-called Russian expert, and I think that because of this long preoccupation with the subject — not despite it, mark you, but precisely because of it — it is time that my ideas, too, were taken thoroughly apart and put together again with relation, this time, to the present scene, and not to all the memories I cherish, and all the ancedotes I have been accustomed to telling, about the earlier years.

Such seminars would not, I think, serve their purpose unless they were the product of very high-level initiative and enthusiasm within the administration. But if that initiative and enthusiasm were there, the institutional facilities to organize and accommodate them would not be hard to find.

# U.S.-SOVIET TRADE, PEACE AND PROSPERITY
## By Donald M. Kendall

I want to tell you why I feel so deeply that it is in America's best interests — and in the interests of world peace — for us to increase our trade and commerce with the Soviet Union.

This, of course, is a sensitive and controversial topic, and many people may wonder why I have come to be such an outspoken advocate of better U.S.-Soviet relations.

I am firmly convinced that increased U.S.-Soviet trade will threaten neither our economic system nor America's defense, but rather increase the chances for world peace, while providing significant commercial benefits.

But I think it is important to put those trade relations in a broader political perspective. It is important because however remunerative such trade may or may not be to individual businesses or other private groups, it has been an integral and significant part of overall U.S. policy toward the Soviet Union as it has developed over the past several years.

The shorthand description for this policy is detente. Detente as a term has picked up a great deal of emotional baggage but, despite some of the rhetoric of the Presidential campaign last year, I want to make clear that it is not a synonym for being soft on the Russians.

There was no doubt in the minds of the framers and practitioners of detente, for example, that the fundamental ideological hostility of the two political systems had not changed, or that there was any foreseeable prospect of such a change. Rather, detente was conceived as a hard-headed policy of realism, based on a recognition of the fact that these hostile systems were likely to have to live side by side in the world for a long, long time and a consequent conviction both of the futility and of the

Donald Kendall, chairman and Executive Officer of PepsiCo, Inc., helped found the U.S.-U.S.S.R. Trade and Economic Council, of which he was the American chairman. His essay is based on an address before the Salt Lake Area Chamber of Commerce on Sept. 15, 1977.

dangers of continuing the attitudes of the Cold War.

Not only was the rhetoric of the Cold War becoming increasingly sterile, but the attempt to score cheap debating points over every incident which arose between the two countries or which affected both carried with it the danger of confrontation and possible nuclear war.

The policy of detente, therefore, was an attempt to construct a fabric of positive relationships, to reduce tensions and antagonisms through concentration on areas of common interest or mutual advantage or on issues where mutually satisfactory resolution was possible. Intergovernmental cooperation to deal with common problems, such as those of environment, health, transportation, cultural exchanges and, importantly, trade relations were promising areas for such positive expanded contact. The result of this effort would be to open dialogue between leading figures of the two countries in a number of functional areas on problems which would encourage a psychological pattern and attitude of cooperation; to develop a web of interlocking relations of mutual value and, in general, to reduce the antagonism and suspicion with which decades of mutual hostility had colored virtually all contacts between the two societies.

Let me emphasize again, that, while a web of mutually advantageous relations might increase Soviet reluctance to act in such a way as to jeopardize them, this policy was not pursued with any idea that the Soviet Union had changed its philosophy and was no longer a threat to the American way of life, or that such a policy would induce such a change. On the contrary, an integral element of detente was the maintenance of military strength second to none and a determination, if our national interests were challenged, to respond strongly, even brutally. The essential point is that the cooperative aspects of detente were designed to ensure that these challenges, if they occurred, did not come about through misunderstanding or inadvertence. Therefore, the twin pillars of detente, as I understand the policy of the past few years, have been to support and encourage responsible Soviet behavior and to react sharply to any Soviet challenge to the national interests of the United States.

## Trade and Detente

The trade picture changed as our total relationship changed and as trade emerged as a major element of the policy of detente. The new era in commercial relations was really inaugurated in 1972 at the famous Moscow Summit Meeting. President Nixon and General Secretary Brezhnev reached agreement on basic principles, which, after several months of negotiation, resulted in the 1972 Trade Agreement.

Under its terms, the Soviets provided greater access to their markets by authorizing U.S. businesses to establish offices in Moscow and liberalizing their visa procedures. Additionally, they made an unusually forthright commitment to avoid foreign market disruption as a result of their exports. A Moscow World Trade Center was also to be constructed in time for the 1980 Olympics.

The United States, for its part, agreed to grant the Soviets what is called Most-Favored-Nation status and normal access to Export-Import Bank credits. This would have lifted the discriminatory tariffs on Soviet exports which were imposed by the Smoot-Hawley tariff schedules developed before the great depression when U.S. protectionism was at its most virulent.

With the signing of the Trade Agreement, President Nixon proceeded to exercise his proper authority and "opened" the Ex-Im Bank window to the Soviet Union for the first time. By the end of 1974, nearly half a billion dollars in Ex-Im credits had been extended to the Soviets. This was a promising beginning, and observers in both countries envisaged the development of a mutually profitable commercial relationship which would undergird an era of detente.

Their hopes were premature. While the President could authorize the extension of Ex-Im credits on his own authority, congressional ratification was required to grant MFN status to the Soviet Union. I'm sure you know the rest of the story: in December of 1974, the so-called Jackson-Vanik Amendment, tacked onto a massive piece of general legislation, tied the granting of MFN to the Soviets' emigration policy. An unlikely collection of well-meaning, but misguided, special interest groups were able to coalesce around support of this amendment which Senator Jackson skillfully exploited to further his own Presidential aspirations.

Almost unnoticed by all except the U.S.S.R. was the Stevenson Amendment to the same Act. This Amendment reduced the level of Ex-Im Bank credits which could be extended to the Soviet Union below those levels then in force with other nations.

The Soviets interpreted this as discrimination and, on top of the Jackson-Vanik Amendment, felt that the United States Congress had reneged on the terms of the 1972 Trade Agreement.

## A Tragic Congressional Decision

The sad irony was that the Soviet authorities, as a result of quiet and patient efforts by the United States, had earlier allowed an unprecedented increase in the number of those permitted to emigrate. By spelling out requirements for emigration in the Trade Act, the U.S. Congress appeared to be legislating the internal affairs of another state, something which the Soviets could not accept.

Quite candidly, I believe the amendments represent a tragic decision by the U.S. Congress. The results of this action speak for themselves: the Jewish emigration rate dropped from a pre-Jackson/Vanik Amendment high of 34,500 to the current rate of about 13,000. Similarly, the bilateral trade that seemed to hold so much promise stagnated — and has remained stagnant.

However sincere our intentions, however pure our motives, the United States cannot take upon itself the job of legislating the internal domestic affairs of other nations. To paraphrase John Adams: We are a friend to all who desire freedom but a guarantor of only our own.

Let me emphasize right now that my strong criticism of Congress on this matter does not indicate a lack of concern for human rights. In fact, I believe that trade is the most effective vehicle for creating an environment in which human rights and other important issues have a better chance of being resolved, and I think our experience with respect to Soviet emigration supports this thesis.

Daniel Yergin of the Harvard Business School put it well in a recent *Foreign Affairs* article: ". . . expanded economic relations do bring about a situation where external forces can have a greater degree of direct and indirect influence on what has been to date a highly insulated political system."

## Soviet Trade and
## The American Economy

In addition to its role in the overall policy of detente, there are a host of sound reasons why it makes good economic sense for the United States to expand its trade with the Soviets. First, and perhaps foremost, is the matter of jobs. Exports provide jobs. The U.S. Commerce Department conservatively estimates that $25,000 in manufactured exports provides one job, while it takes $42,000 in agricultural exports to do the same thing. If left to develop on its own, unrestricted by artificial restraints, U.S.-Soviet trade could grow to several billions of dollars per year and generate hundreds of thousands of American jobs.

Secondly, American trade with the Soviets — and with all of Eastern Europe for that matter — has favorably affected the U.S. balance of payments. From 1971 to 1976, the United States experienced a $2.5 billion favorable trade balance with the Soviet Union — $3.0 billion for all of Eastern Europe.

With this country's trade and total foreign payments slipping ever more dramatically out of balance, due in large part to soaring energy expenditures, we cannot afford to ignore the benefits this profitable bilateral trade affords.

The fact of the matter is that the Soviets have tremendous economic needs which the United States is in an excellent position to help meet. Our highly advanced agricultural technology makes farm products the biggest proportion — over 60 percent — of U.S. exports to the Soviet Union. While agricultural products will continue to be extremely important in the two-way trade, it is in the export of manufactured products that I feel the greatest potential lies.

In the past, Soviet economic growth had been predicated on expansion of the labor force and the capital stock, but the emphasis now is on growth based on increased productivity. In fact, the tenth five-year plan discussed and approved by the Soviet hierarchy in 1976 is billed as the plan of "efficiency and quality."

In order to achieve the goals of this plan, the Soviet Union must rely heavily on the importation of technology and high-technology products from the Western world. They are very clear about this, but they are equally clear about their intentions to make their purchases — as they should — on the most favorable possible terms.

Unfortunately, because of Congress, the United States cannot extend government credits to the Soviets through the Ex-Im Bank as we do to our other trading partners, and our terms, therefore, are not the most favorable. We are thus losing significant export opportunities to nations such as West Germany, Japan, Italy and France whose governments have adopted a much more enlightened view in this matter.

In some cases, American affiliates overseas are being offered host-country government credit assistance and guarantees and are undertaking to sell technologically advanced systems to the Soviet Union.

With know-how from the Kellogg Company, for example, more than 20 fertilizer plants are presently being built in Japan, at a cost of $700 million, for shipment to and assembly in the Soviet Union. But the jobs — and the profits — are going to the Japanese who are granting the necessary credits. GE technology is responsible for a big $250 million gas line compressor project now underway in the Soviet Union. But again, the benefits are going elsewhere — to the Italians and the French in this case.

## U.S. Shortsightedness

U.S. shortsightedness in the area of government financing is really a double-edged sword. By abdicating our competitive advantage to the other industrialized nations, we are foregoing current earnings and giving away future market position as well.

As if that were not enough, companies which want to do business in the Soviet Union are having to fight another rear-guard action at home with those who see dire results if we sell our technology to the Soviets. We have laws designed to protect the sale of purely military technology, and I am all in favor of protecting those few areas where our technology gives us a military advantage. But as a general rule, I do not believe that knowledge can be contained by national boundaries.

If we will not permit the Soviets access to our know-how, then they will turn to the Japanese or the Germans or the Italians to get what they need. We have no monopoly on information here, though some people may think we do. As a matter of fact, if Americans had been denied the benefit of technological advances generated in other countries, this nation would be in a pretty sorry state. The gasoline and diesel engine, for example, were invented in Germany, as were the electron microscope and the geiger counter. England gave us the steam locomotive, jet engine and the besemer process for producing steel. The telescope came from Holland, the telegraph from Italy, the gyroscope from France; and the list goes on.

The additional fear some have — that, once they have our technology, the Soviets will soon be competing with us in world markets — is just not realistic. Their internal needs are so vast that any technological advances and productivity gains they make from the importation of American know-how will be devoted to domestic requirements for the foreseeable future.

In saying all this, I do not want to give the impression that all is bleak in U.S.-Soviet commercial relations. Some progress — though very modest — has been, and is being, made. Since 1970, the two-way trade has increased from a paltry $179 million to over $2.5 billion. This is only as large as our trade with tiny Peru or Belgium.

There has also been a significant increase in communication. Twenty-two U.S. companies now have representative offices in Moscow. And the U.S.-USSR Trade and Economic Council, which I chair for the American side, has facilitated thousands of business contacts and sponsored dozens of Soviet trade delegation visits to this country.

## Trade and Human Rights

Additionally, the 1972 Trade Agreement is not dead — both sides have had the good sense not to kill it — it is just in a state of suspended animation. It could be implemented if the Congress would see its way clear to ratify the terms negotiated five years ago, by untying the grant of Most-Favored-Nation status to Soviet emigration and by permitting the extension of Ex-Im Bank credits on the same terms as to other nations.

This does not mean America would foreclose the opportunity to take stands on human rights or other sensitive matters. The final Act of the Conference on European Security and Cooperation — better known as the Helsinki Accord —was ratified in 1975 by the United States, the Soviet Union and 33 other nations and includes procedures for one signatory nation to take another to task for lack of adherence to the terms of the Agreement. This Accord provides an excellent vehicle for pursuit of American interests in the human rights issue.

I do not believe that advances in trade and economic cooperation should be held hostage to equal advances in the human rights areas. Progress in one area will significantly improve the overall climate so that the chances for progress in other, more sensitive, areas will be enhanced.

The overall thought I would like to leave with you is that we must think in realistic and dispassionate terms about the Soviet Union. We must never underestimate the depth of the ideological gulf between us, and we must never fail to react strongly and swiftly to any challenge. At the same time, with no illusion that if we only show goodwill the Soviet leaders will begin to behave like us, we should work with them to develop areas of mutual interest, such as trade, to build habits of restraint, patterns of coexistence, and, perhaps, eventually even cooperation.

This combination of toughness and encouragement toward responsible and cooperative behavior is the best hope for peace in the world and for the preservation and extension of the values we hold dear.

# THE ARMS RACE AND AMERICAN POLITICS
## By John Kenneth Galbraith

T he subject of American-Soviet relations is one that invites the worst tendencies in our political literature — apocalyptic vision, the elaborately torrid phrase, discovery of deeply sinister motive. The excuse for the first two is better here than on most occasions; the issues under discussion are, all too literally, ones of life and death. I would like to see, nonetheless, if it is possible to speak of them in a reasonably calm voice. I would like to see if the politics of detente can be discussed without trying too deliberately to open wounds, old or new.

The case for detente I take to be simple. It is not to love or be loved, important as these may be. It is to have a relationship with the Soviet Union which allows us to negotiate arrangements that ensure the survival of both states and the people in between. That extensive, perhaps nearly total destruction of life would be the consequence of war I believe there is now no serious scientific doubt. George McGovern, in an article in *The Progressive,* adduced information that some might survive such an exchange in the Southern Hemisphere — to die later, because of a depleted ozone layer, from sunburn and cancer. It might not be worthwhile. A year and a half ago I visited Cheyenne Mountain near Colorado Springs — our command post in case of nuclear war. The tunnels extend a mile or two into the mountain; the ultimate inner control rooms are mounted on springs to absorb the shock of a nearby thermonuclear strike. There are stocks of food and water. Also some reading matter. The people therein estimate that they might last for six weeks longer than those outside. It would not, one would think, be a time for pleasant reflection.

The great weight of informed opinion holds, I believe, that the people of the Soviet Union, and those who make decisions there, are as aware of the

*Professor Galbraith, the Harvard economist, was Ambassador to India and is author of numerous books. His most recent book is The Age of Uncertainty. Mr. Galbraith's presentation here is based on an address before the Soviet-American Conference, sponsored by the National Democratic Forum, June 6, 1977.*

realities of nuclear conflict as we. They were educated by a much more horrifying experience in two wars than were we. Few, if any, who have had occasion to discuss these matters with responsible Russians have retained doubts as to the depths of their anxiety. They also know that the ashes of Communism and those of capitalism would be indistinguishable — and lost therein would be all the heritage in knowledge, art and civilization of 5,000 years. All at the press of a button.

No one can doubt the existence of a contrary opinion: Communists are ruthlessly ambitious, utterly perfidious and hopelessly suicidal. So they will risk anything in the hope of preserving a few of their own. This irrationality is a force in our politics. It is brought to the support of economic interest and the fears which are a prime factor in the political alignment on detente. I shall proceed, however, on the assumption, made I believe by all informed people, that the Soviets seek, as do we, a measure of safety in life.

## The Republicans and the Democrats

It follows from what I've just said that the arms race with its threat to survival is not an ideological conflict. It is a trap in which technological innovation on one side forces responding and superseding innovation and investment on the other. There will be no escape except in a context that allows discussion and negotiation. I have no doubt that there are ways by which Soviet attitudes and internal politics could be improved to facilitate this end. About this, as about the other shortcomings of Soviet society and behavior, we can do very little. We *can* understand our own political alignment, and that is my present concern.

The politics of our relations with the Soviet Union cross party lines and occupational and class interests and are singularly indifferent to all. We must recognize, I believe, that the Republicans now have a reputation for handling these relations more resourcefully, imaginatively and prudently than do we Democrats. The test is that, had that performance, not economics, been the central issue in the last election, they would have won. The task of our party is to show that we are more progressive and prudent than our opponents. What is the alignment with which we have to deal?

Favoring detente is the largest and most potent force in the American polity — one that is relatively amorphous and voiceless except at election time or when deeply aroused. It is the force that has punished our party so reliably in the past, and for wars both just and unjust. It combines an instinctive pacifism with, in the present case, a strong and rational belief that some reasonable working relationship with the Soviets is essential if we are to avoid reciprocal suicide. These were the people who expressed themselves in that prolonged cheer when, during his Inaugural address, President Carter held out the hope of a world set free from the nuclear terror. They are the people who have now taught all who seek office that a mere mention of the use of nuclear weapons means political euthanasia. One remembers the accidental, and I think unjust, misfortune of Barry Goldwater in 1964 and the later well-earned one of Curtis LeMay.

We do not, characteristically, have a name for this vast political constituency. I do not think anyone can be in doubt that it is a force of great power. It mobilizes slowly. It is hard to see and hear. But it votes relentlessly.

In support of this large but amorphous power are other interests, all much less important. The most alert is the scientific community. We now know that the closer men live to nuclear terror, the more terrified, not surprisingly, they become. The scientists in both countries, to their great credit, have led in the search for accommodation. There are those too with an economic interest in Soviet trade. This I do not believe to be very important except, perhaps, in a year of grain shortages and big Soviet wheat purchases. Foreign trade, the old South in earlier times apart, has always been small in the American political calculation and influence, and trade with the Soviet Union is small in the present total. Those who resist making our trade relations equitable as between the Soviets and other countries believe this trade an important bargaining chip. It is not. I would like to see such an equitable relationship but I think the issue has far more symbolic than economic importance.

There is also a community that is interested in the continuing and irrepressible cultural and literary achievements of Russians. Artists, alas, are also politically unimportant. Least important of all is the small surviving handful of Communists who make the case for a close and supportive association with the Soviet Union. They are not entirely unimportant, for they still remind some nervous souls that this was once a perilous stand to take.

## The Political Support for Detente

Overwhelmingly the political support for detente lies with an acute sense of its relation to the desire to exist. That is the political force; all else is, in a sense, peripheral.

The opposition to detente is much more complex. It is also better disguised by euphemism. And it involves me in more problems of clear expression, for it is not a case that I am accustomed to make.

Its most important base is economic interest. Tension with the Soviets sustains our largest public bureaucracy and, in aggregate terms, one of our largest industries. They are a bureaucracy and industry that attract notably innovative, intelligent and articulate people. It is in connection with bureaucratic and economic interest that euphemism enters; we have here what is by all odds our most elaborate exercise in evasive word and thought.

That there is an economic interest in the arms race no one in ordinary conversation denies. No one would wish to be thought quite that naive. But to admit this publicly is never thought permissible; to say that the arms race is good because it sustains income and employment, adds usefully to innovation and gross national product, verges on the obscene. We all know that, at budget time, Soviet power and perfidy show a sharp seasonal increase. None can doubt tension is helpful for the war industry. But these things we do not say. I do not suggest that deliberate legerdemain is involved. The mind is an accommodating thing; it adjusts readily to need. The great corporate executive is deeply committed in his opposition to government intervention until the day when his bankers tell him he must get help from Washington or else. Then belief is reconciled with financial need. You must know how easily, as an economist, one learns to reconcile the actual development with earlier false prediction. People disguise economic interest from themselves by the requisite alternative belief the more successfully, the more directly involved. And the rest of us do not like to think that, as a nation, we risk potential suicide for present economic advantage.

It would greatly clarify our political discussion if economic interest could be openly recognized and discussed. It would help the discussion if those who are on the other side — my side — could deal with it as a fact of life and not as something calling automatically for lofty indignation. This has also prevented proper discussion of economic alternatives — alternatives that go beyond a vacuous statement of the need, the form in which I am forced to dismiss the issue today. It would be an appropriate return if those primarily interested in the economic gains from tension would stop taking refuge behind such words as peace, freedom and national security. Also no one much is fooled.

Supporting economic interest are the two great fears that, in the past, have pervaded our political life. Perhaps they have been as powerful as economic interest or more so: One is the fear of Communism; the other is the fear of being thought soft on Communism. The first fear is deeply indigenous to the conservative soul. It seems likely, however, that it is in decline. There can hardly be doubt that modern socialism, not less than modern capitalism, faces rather intractable problems of economic management. Were socialism as certain and easy of success as was thought in the last century, all the world would be socialist now.

We have learned also that industrial society, as it develops, is relentlessly plural. No class or occupational or political group can have a monopoly of power — a problem with which the Soviets struggle and which Italian, French and Spanish Communists increasingly concede.

## The Unique Affliction of Liberals

The second fear, that of being thought soft on Communism, is, of course, the unique affliction of liberals. Of the two fears it is by far the more dangerous. Few people in modern times rise to such a dangerous level of irrationality as the liberal who feels that he must show that he is as tough on the Reds as anybody. It is because they are exempt from this fear that conservatives, in recent times, have made more progress in lowering tension than our own political co-religionists. I hope that that affliction, too, is coming to an end.

There are three other sources of tension in our politics where the Soviets are concerned. One is the fear that they are taking over the underdeveloped world. Last year Angola, this year Ethiopia. I do not take this seriously. We have learned to our cost and sorrow that we cannot guide political and economic development in countries distant geographically and culturally from our own. And in China, Ghana, Algeria, Egypt and perhaps Indonesia, the Soviets must surely have learned the same. It is unimaginable that Africans will exchange Portuguese, British or French colonial rule for that of Russia. These countries will search for short cuts to development and affluence. Socialism will seem to be one. This, unhappily for the countries concerned, is not the case. Marx was not wrong when he held that socialism was irrelevant until there was something to socialize. Perhaps the Chinese will prove the contrary; of all nations they have the longest experience in organization, the scarce resource for large-scale public experiment. I cannot think that anyone would wish the Russians the misfortune of having to take responsibility for the success of a seriously Communist Republic of Ethiopia.

There is also in our politics the sensitive issue of Israel. A few years ago one would worry about a confrontation in the Middle East which would bring us automatically to the side of the Israelis, the Soviets as automatically to the Arabs'. Not everything in our diplomacy fails. In recent years we have done something, perhaps much, to persuade the Arab states that our commitment to the Israelis is combined with a commitment to peaceful settlement. In consequence, the number of people who feel that to be for Israel requires them to be against the Soviets and a Soviet/Arab alliance is almost certainly declining. I hope that that continues; it alone allows us to work usefully for tranquility in the region.

Finally, there is the issue of human rights. Let me assure all that my stand for free expression in all forms is impeccable — on occasion, I've been thought, however wrongly, to enjoy even its more abrasive exercise. But I have never been as alarmed by this as a threat to detente as some of my friends. That is because civil and human rights are in such poor condition in so many places.

Complaint of their perversion in the Soviet Union was certain sooner or later to be lost in comment on their abuse elsewhere in the world. Also our role can only be hortatory, and there is an unfortunate discontinuity between hortatory effort by one country and the result in the country advised. There have, in fact, been only two countries where, in recent years, we have been in a position, by our actual presence, to exercise immediate, direct leverage on behalf of human rights. There alone could we expect results. The results were not great. The two countries were South

Vietnam and South Korea.

Such, then, is the political alignment on easing tension, making possible the context in which we negotiate with the Soviets for safety and survival. All could be helped by the tactful recognition by Soviet leaders that such is the balance of forces. Such recognition I believe to be important and something to be urged. Our diplomacy, to the extent that it can be informed, should be maturely conscious of the forces in the Soviet Union that seek an easing of tension. The Soviets, one may surely urge, should be cautious in action that adds to political tension here.

Can one be sanguine? When Democrats are in power, there is always the danger that those intrinsically interested in tension, in combination with scared liberalism — liberalism that lives in terror of seeming to appease — will cause overreaction. That was the coalition that put — and kept — us in Indo-China. But we do learn. Because it is amorphous, the political interest in lowered tension, rational negotiation and ultimate survival responds very much more slowly. But, if often latent, that interest is strongly there. And it does respond. I wish that that response might be faster. But no one should doubt its power, and least of all those who wish to survive in public offices.

# THE DANGER OF THE HUMAN RIGHTS CAMPAIGN
## By David Riesman

The concepts of human rights and human prospects suggest the possibility of conflicts among our ideals, that is, the possibility that the proclaimed goal of human rights may inadvertently risk the human prospects of survival itself. This is the risk of immediate destruction through what I have regarded, since Hiroshima, as the overarching danger to the species: the existence of nuclear weapons and the possibility to which these give rise of an escalating nuclear conflict among the super-powers. I supported the candidacy of President Carter on a number of grounds, chief among them the fact that he is the first president with a technical understanding of those weapons and with a serious and systematic interest in controlling and eventually banishing them — an effort that must begin between the Soviet Union and ourselves before we can hope to restrain proliferation among those other nations who now possess such weapons in actuality or potential.

At the same time, in lending his prestige and immense moral capital to the campaign for human rights vis-a-vis the Soviet Union, it is possible that President Carter has jeopardized his hopes on the all-important nuclear front, not only because prominent officialdom in the Soviet Union says so, but because of the long-run impact of the Carter campaign on *American* public opinion. Indeed, it is difficult to predict the possible impact of the human rights campaign, not so much on the vocal dissidents who have already suffered jeopardy, but on the generally silent but nonetheless in the long run influential public opinion of non-elites in the Soviet Union and its uneasy satellites.

*David Riesman, Professor of Sociology at Harvard and author of* The Lonely Crowd, *is a pioneer in the effort to focus social science critiques on American foreign policy. His article is based on excerpts from his Commencement Address at Williams College in June, 1977, which were published in* Commonweal *(Nov. 11, 1977) and* Society *(November-December, 1977).*

The campaign for human rights vis-a-vis the Soviet Union of course did not begin with President Carter. In one sense it goes back to the very beginning of the Soviet regime, while long before that the insistence of many Americans on the proper moral conduct of other countries was a factor in launching us into both the Spanish-American War and the First World War. The contemporary campaign vis-a-vis the Soviet Union would seem to take its origin at the conclusion of the fighting in Vietnam, and, in some degree, to represent the unliquidated continuation of the American domestic conflict over that war by other means and with somewhat altered partisans.

Liberal intellectuals, public officials, and interest groups ranging from influential American Zionists to longshoremen to the hard-liners who run the international division of the AFL-CIO have been in the forefront of the human rights issue, in some part as an attack on the efforts to achieve detente by former President Nixon and Henry Kissinger — an attack joined by the Republican Cold War Right, and the Democratic-liberal Left with its call for an open moral diplomacy, superior to realpolitik. The campaign appeals to our idealism: to our hope of living in a world without torture, without slavery, one where people are free to speak and to move about — although the current campaign against illegal immigrants and, indeed, against any further immigration at all fits in badly with a desire for greater freedom of movement across frontiers.

## Competing Ideals

It is not sufficient argument against our human rights campaign that we ourselves often violate our own ideals in practice vis-a-vis immigration of other people. On another level we attempt to limit or keep out, through ever increasing efforts at protectionism, the importation of goods which others can make more efficiently than we. The purpose of an ideal is to express something not easily achieved. No American policy, foreign or domestic, is viable which rests on a definition of the national interest — a questionable concept — which fails to take account of our national idealism; the problem is to adjudicate among competing ideals.

The notion that ideals may not be compatible with each other is often difficult for Americans to accept; we are inclined to believe that all good things are compatible, that we can have *both* human survival and human rights without any risk to the former or compromise or delay with respect to the latter. Furthermore, the focus on human rights, though now voiced by a generally liberal Democratic administration, inevitably plays into the never wholly defeated Cold War mentality of ethnocentric and patrioteering Americans even while President Carter is seeking to open up our relations with Cuba and Panama, with Vietnam and even with North Korea.

The current generation of young people has not grown up with nightmares of the possibility of nuclear devastation. Vietnam was not seen as an issue of nuclear peril, as it was for me, but as a moral outrage and, for many, a personal threat and a personal moral dilemma.

My generation is the product of a different history. I did not share a number of attitudes that prevailed in this country during the Second World War. I never for a moment had any sympathy for Stalinism, and I regarded Soviet brutalities as quite as murderous as Hitler's. Yet, despite my fear lest Hitler emerge victorious, I believed at the time and still do that the British and American bombing of Dresden and Hamburg, as well as Tokyo and other large Japanese cities, transcended the limits which need to be placed on warfare and was not necessary for Allied survival. . . .

Still, terrible as these mass bombings were, carried on with so-called conventional weapons, the use of nuclear bombs at Hiroshima and Nagasaki marked a perilous dividing line. In the decades since then I have fought those supposed realists like Edward Teller and many strategists who, pointing out that the largest conventional weapons were more deadly than the smallest nuclear ones, sought to erase the formal line between nuclear war and all other kinds of war. The idea, toyed with in Vietnam, that one could use tactical nuclear weapons, seemed a dangerous delusion; things generally go wrong with such calculations, and escalation to mutual annihilation could be the likely result.

## A Feeling of Deja Vu

There have been many agonizing moments over the last thirty years in which hopes for rapprochement were shattered by internal politics of the Soviet Union or of the United States. Or just as a meeting was planned to discuss the end of nuclear testing, and the possibility of controlling nuclear weapons, something accidental prevented it — for example, the U-2 spy flight (which may not have been accidental, but undertaken by those prepared to risk and hence perhaps torpedo, the forthcoming summit meeting between Khrushchev and Eisenhower). In this context President Carter's raising of the human rights issue at the same time that he hoped to assure success of the SALT talks gives a feeling of deja vu.

Tribalism within nation-states and among nation-states remains the most powerful force at work in the world today, more powerful even than class conflicts although especially powerful when tribal and class divisions coincide. The recent American presidential election was fought along both lines of fission. When I became an early supporter of candidate Jimmy Carter, I found myself opposed by many on the grounds of both regional and religious tribalism — by people with no understanding of or sympathy with the complexities of southern theological traditions and suspicious of white southerners in general. Yet as C. Vann Woodward pointed out a number of years ago, white southerners are the only major American group to have suffered military defeat, and at least in some instances are therefore likely to have a sense of limits of tragedy. This has not been a general American characteristic, not even a southern one.

But President Carter is as American as he is southern. He has an all-American faith that problems are soluble and that they can be resolved not only within but among nations, especially when talked about candidly and openly. Candor can be both right conduct and successful strategy. Yet to believe that it will always work seems to me an often unconscious ethnocentric failure to appreciate that we cannot approach other countries in the same way that at times, in our cults of intimacy and of sharing, in our demolishing of the line between public and private, we approach each other both in adversary journalism and in many aspects of personal life.

The fact that the Soviet Union lacks adversary journalism (except in *Samizdat* or the privately circulated writings of dissidents) and is not an open society has been a stumbling block in the efforts to secure a test ban treaty which would cover underground testing, since our negotiators insisted at the time of negotiation of the 1963 partial test ban treaty that it would be impossible without such inspection to distinguish between an underground test and an earthquake. This was a mistaken and even tendentious judgment: the best seismic experts believe that a distinction is easily made between an underground test and an earthquake; moreover, our spy satellites and our intelligence can tell us what is going on in the Soviet Union, even though we do not always want to reveal how much we know because that will tip off the Soviet Union as to how we know it. But above all, any analysis of this sort must distinguish between capabilities and intentions. Much of our thinking about the Soviet Union, like that of military men professionally, has been "worst case" thinking — a mode of thinking which can be self-confirming since it creates an alliance of the supposedly patriotic war party inside the United States with the patriotic war party within the Soviet Union, against the civilian population of both countries.

Again to underline the fact that Jimmy Carter did not begin but is in fact trying to curb the American temptation to worst case thinking, we should recall the fact that candidate John Kennedy made the utterly fictitious "missile gap" the main theme of his attack on candidate Richard Nixon and the previous Republican administration — indeed, later at the time of the Cuban missile crisis, he did what no other American president has done: endangered the planet in order to force Premier Khrushchev to back down. He created a crisis situation out of the Soviet missiles in Cuba, an issue that could have been handled more safely over time, since in reality the United States was no more threatened by these missiles in Cuba (over which Soviet control was maintained) than by those ICBMs already in place or potentially located in offshore submarines. The relatively conciliatory Khrushchev, who had been the first openly to admit to the crimes of the Stalin era, was forced out of office by his internal enemies, in part as a result of this. But in the finest act of his presidency, John Kennedy got the Joint Chiefs of Staff and other crucial "hard-line" groups not to oppose the partial test ban treaty of 1963 .

## A Perilous Campaign

The history of our relations with the Soviet Union over the control of nuclear weapons is a history of might-have-beens. When President Eisenhower, in what was for him an uncharacteristic act of boyish openness, accepted responsibility for the U-2 overflight, one possible moment of rapprochement was lost. Now Brezhnev may be forced out of office by his illness, giving still further power to other factions in the Soviet military-industrial complex, before a new SALT agreement has been reached.

It is in this situation that the launching of the human rights campaign against the Soviet Union seems so perilous. It was not begun by candidate or President Carter. It has been carried on by Senator Jackson and others in the Senate — and Senator Jackson is a man who, contrary to widespread cynicism, is not only the "Senator from Boeing Aircraft," but also a true believer in human rights, as are many other idealistic Americans. And just as Senator Jackson had been mistaken in insisting that the Soviet Union would on materialistic grounds accept our trade terms while accepting also our vocal criticism concerning the emigration of Jewish dissidents, so President Carter began his administration by insisting that the Soviet Union would come to terms on the SALT agreements because the USSR would so clearly gain by it (as we would also) while at the same time insisting on its accepting our standards of human rights as well.

Meantime, the Senate has already indicated where it stands by its vote of considerably less than two-thirds in favor of the confirmation of Paul Warnke as our disarmament negotiator. And the human rights issue itself vis-a-vis the Soviet Union can be taken up readily by the Congress to use against the President, who is himself now inclined to be more cautious on the issue — in other words, to use against a SALT agreement, as an all too easy argument to add to other arguments. In fact, the judgment of many experts is that we are more than amply protected by the mobile and dispersed weapons we already possess. By giving the movement for human rights full legitimacy at an earlier point, President Carter may have lost the ability to control and focus it.

But I now must enter an area where I can claim no expertise: that of the internal politics of the Soviet Union — yet an area where I am guided by a certain skepticism bred by experience with American Sovietologists going back to the 1930s. I had the odd experience, during the height of the Cold War in the middle and late 1950s, of being told that I was "soft on communism" by people whom I had known when they were Communists, Trotskyites, Schachtmanites, and so on, and when I was, as I have remained, convinced of the brutality, corruption, and — in many areas —

sheer incompetence of Soviet society. Some of these Russian experts were among the last to realize what Victor Zorza had long been pointing out: the likelihood of a Sino-Soviet split in what had been thought of as monolithic world communism. More important, the Soviet Union suffers even more from internal tribalism than we do, with many nationalities struggling to get out from under the control of the Great Russians, and in which the countries of the Eastern zone produce superior consumer goods and have a higher standard of living, despite having constantly to pay tribute to the Soviet Union, than do the citizens of the latter.

## The Necessity for Restraint

I am not contending that Soviet citizens are ready to break out in open revolt, but rather that Soviet authorities see themselves as beleaguered by China, West Germany and the especially threatening dangers of French and Italian communism in Western Europe (threatening because they are not under Soviet hegemony), and then of course by the United States. The Soviet Union has never been able to achieve the kind of disciplined work force and the internalized as well as superficial obedience that the Chinese Communists appear to have been able to instill, drawing in part on long Confucian and other traditions. Hence, the fact that the Soviets have a long tradition of superiority in artillery, and that they can make and no doubt deliver huge bombs, is as much a sign of defensiveness as aggression — indeed, their foreign policy in recent years has brought a series of defeats — even though their defensiveness, in dialectic with ours, may, in the form of nuclear war, end their prospects and ours.

This outlook has meant (for me, at least) a necessary restraint in criticism of the Soviet Union, even while prior to today's era there remained in this country quite a few influential intellectuals and writers who, as currently in many European countries, blinded themselves to the cruelties of the regime because it called itself socialist and because of their awareness of the evils of their own nation-states. And today I am in a position of deep moral ambiguity because, on the one hand, I admire enormously the courage of the Soviet dissidents, whatever their personal ideologies, and share many of the values that inspire someone like the scientist Sakharov; but at the same time I have consistently refused to sign petitions or in any other way lend my name to the criticisms of the treatment of these dissidents. In a bipolar nuclear world we cannot afford to hold to a simple, straightforward, universalistic moral standard such as one might hope for in a world free of the threat of mass annihilation.

There are many students of the Soviet Union who would disagree with my analysis, who believe that the regime is fully effective, secure, and unthreatened, that its leaders only pretend to be stung by criticism — criticisms which are justified in any circumstances other than nuclear peril at the very moment when we are trying to reach across that chasm for some understanding. My position on human rights does not spring from cultural or moral relativism. While one must take account of local conditions, and of the perils and priorities of other peoples, that does not mean that one condones ancient Aztec human sacrifice or today's tribal murders in Bangladesh. To repeat: it is because I see the nuclear question as always foremost that I cannot be sanguine about the human prospect in the long run, unless the human rights issue of the moment in this country is made less salient.

# DOOMSDAY SCENARIOS AND THE CHALLENGE TO SALT

## By G. B. Kistiakowsky

Thirty years after the start of the cold war, the United States and the Soviet Union still live in a state of uncertainty and insecurity. In America, this condition has been attributed from the start to the aggressiveness of Soviet Communism, which is seen as striving for world hegemony and bent on the destruction of its principal obstacle, the United States. In Moscow, just as consistently, the guilt has been assigned to the evil designs of American militarism and imperialism.

Today, in facing the consequences of this confrontation, we Americans are at a crossroads. Depending on which road we take, we may win, or lose, one of those rare opportunities in modern times to bring a measure of stability to an increasingly dangerous world.

For five years now, an interim agreement known among the experts as SALT I has limited the number of strategic land- and sea-based ballistic-missile launchers on each side. The agreement expired last October, and although both sides have promised to continue abiding by its provisions, the self-restraint this requires, in the absence of a new formal agreement, could well erode fairly soon. For waiting in the wings on both sides are new types of strategic weapons — bigger and more accurate ICBM's with multiple warheads, some even mobile, and the long-range air-, land-and sea-based cruise missiles. Many of these new weapons are clearly capable of more than a deterrent or defensive mission, and are, therefore, provocative by nature. Others are difficult to detect by reconnaissance satellites, and thus add to the other side's sense of insecurity. Some are destabilizing in both ways.

The Soviet-American negotiations for a new agreement — SALT II — that were resumed last spring have been making headway, but accord is

George Kistiakowsky, Professor of Chemistry emeritus at Harvard, was Assistant for Science and Technology to President Eisenhower and an early proponent of arms negotiations. His article here was originally published in the New York Times Magazine, Nov. 27, 1977.

still blocked by a number of technically complex issues. President Carter, Secretary of State Cyrus Vance and Arms Control Director Paul Warnke have all shown a clear understanding of the dire protential consequences of the arms race and have given arms control new priority on their agenda. Yet, despite the urgency of the situation, the Aministration's policy, and the narrowness of the gap that separates the parties to the talks, there is real danger that no agreement will be reached — or, if reached, that it will not be ratified by the Senate.

Why?

Part of the answer has to do with the technicalities of missile performance, and with differences between the strategic doctrines and negotiating tactics of the two sides. But another, and perhaps the major, reason, is to be found in the domestic politics of arms control.

## Cold War Voices

Once again, as so often in the past, there are powerful voices in this country urging intensification of the cold war and rejection of efforts at moderation — efforts that are construed as serving Moscow's aggressive designs. Once again, we are asked to determine our actions not in the light of our demonstrated ability to more than compensate for any Soviet military advance, but, rather, in response to imaginings, fueled by fears, as to what the Soviets *might* do. This, lamentably, has been the pattern of our decisions on weapon acquisitions and arms control since World War II. To understand it, we must go back to the beginnings of the nuclear age.

While the origins of the cold war are too complex to go into here, it is undeniable that, by the end of the 1940's political positions in Washington and Moscow had hardened. West Berlin was under Soviet blockade; the Korean War was only months away; the United States was heavily committed against Communist insurgency in Greece; and, in Congress, the House Un-American Activities Committee was riding high. Stalin's extreme secretiveness at home, and his iron curtain on the world, kept the Truman Administration guessing about Soviet military capabilities and foreign policy objectives. Diplomatic negotiations were at a standstill. Then, in September 1949, the first Soviet atom bomb shattered American illusions of a prolonged United States monopoly in atomic weapons.

In January 1950, President Truman ordered a speedup on research on the hydrogen bomb and asked for a secret reassessment of our defense and foreign posture. The resulting paper — N.S.C. 68 — made predictions that were nothing short of apocalyptic in substance and tone. "It is quite clear ... that the Kremlin seeks to bring the free world under its dominion," wrote the authors of the report; being "inescapably militant," the Soviet Union "seeks to impose its absolute authority over the rest of the world"; and so on. Given its grim conclusions, which had strong impact on government policy and fed the country's apprehensive political mood, the paper naturally urged a sizable increase in the country's military budget. With the additional stimulus of the Korean War, military budgets rose from $15 billion in 1949 to $50 billion in 1953.

Though much of this money was spent fighting in South Korea's defense, a good portion went to a general build-up of military strength, and especially of the Strategic Air Command. Fragmentary and flimsy intelligence about Soviet bomber forces was characterized by Air Force partisans as evidence of a disastrous "bomber gap." The result was a great buildup of our nuclear-armed heavy-bomber forces — first of the B-47, and then of the intercontinental B-52. Some years later, it was generally agreed that the Soviet heavy-bomber force was modest in size, and that the "bomber gap" was a myth. But, by then, another "gap" was in the making.

In 1957, a top secret study group (the Gaither panel) reported to President Eisenhower that, according to the latest intelligence, the Soviet threat would "become critical by 1959 or early 1960," since, by then, the U.S.S.R. would "acquire significant ICBM delivery capability with megaton warheads." Once again, the White House was urged to increase military spending — and, in addition, to initiate a multibillion-dollar civil-defense program to counter a similar program attributed to the Soviet Union.

President Eisenhower took unkindly to most of the report's recommendations. But the contents were leaked to the press, and, in the summer of 1959, the syndicated columnist Joseph Alsop argued for the existence of a "missile gap." Secretary of Defense Thomas Gates denied the existence of this new gap, but Senator John F. Kennedy used the issue effectively against the Republicans in his 1960 Presidential campaign. And although Kennedy learned upon entering the White House that the "missile gap" was indeed a myth, he had our Minuteman and Polaris strategic-missile programs greatly enlarged in compliance with his campaign promises.

## Arms Race Myths

The real missile gap, in point of fact, had been in our favor. This advantage over the Soviets continued on an increasing scale well into the 1960's. It probably was a factor in Nikita Khrushchev's 1962 decision to deploy medium-range missiles in Cuba — and it certainly was a factor in his subsequent compliance with American demands to remove the still not operational missiles from the island. In the aftermath of this fearful crisis, the Soviet Union embarked on a buildup of its own strategic missile forces, both land-and submarine-based. A decade later, these Soviet forces were substantially larger numerically (in terms of launchers, not warheads) than those of the United States. This massive Soviet program was underestimated by Secretary of Defense Robert McNamara and overestimated by his successor, Melvin Laird.

The shifts in numerical strength had been accompanied by shifts in strategic doctrine. The American doctrine of massive retaliation, devised when the United States still had a virtual monopoly of nuclear weapons, was succeeded in the early 1960's by the concept of "mutual deterrence" The reasoning was that, by that time, both the United States and the Soviet Union knew, beyond any doubt, that each had the means to visit on the other a degree of destruction exceeding anything that any government could accept. The American program projected a force of 1,000 land-based Minuteman ICBM's; 54 of the larger but older land-based Titan II ICBM's; 41 Polaris submarines deploying a total of 656 missiles, and a fleet of B-52's and other heavy bombers — an arsenal considered powerful enough to assure "unacceptable damage" to the Soviet Union (and/or China) even after a surprise Soviet or Chinese nuclear attack.

In spite of that, there were suggestions at several junctures during the 1960's — indeed, they took on the proportions of public campaigns — that Soviet weapons development might have rendered our capability for "assured destruction" inadequate to the task — and, hence, that deterrence might fail.

First came stories about a rapid expansion of the Soviet civil-defense program — measures that would give the Soviet population added protection against  any retaliatory American strike, and that would therefore make the option of a Soviet first strike more tempting to the Soviet leaders.

Then came reports that our intelligence-gathering satellites had spotted a ring of antimissile defenses (ABM's) around Moscow, as well as signs of another ABM system being deployed in other parts of the Soviet Union. To Pentagon officials dedicated to the "worst-case" approach to uncertain intelligence data — what is the worst that the potential enemy is capable of doing to us? — these sightings raised the specter of a country-wide Soviet missile-defense system. The following sequence of events was thereupon envisaged: The Soviets could launch a first strike; those of our missiles that survived this attack would be launched against their Soviet targets; yet most of the retaliatory American warheads would be unable to penetrate the Soviet air-defense system; and the damage inflicted by the few that did penetrate the Soviet shield would not be "unacceptably" severe. Expectations of this outcome would make the Soviet leaders confident of their military superiority.

Though rejected on available evidence by more objective American analysts, this projection was a major factor in the decision to develop a new missile system — MIRV's. Each MIRV (Multiple Independently Targetable Re-entry Vehicle) would be equipped with several warheads; each warhead could be released at a separate target; the new system would multiply the warhead count of an American retaliatory strike and overwhelm the best air defense the Soviets could put up.

## MIRV and SALT

While the MIRV's were being developed, however, new and clearer evidence indicated that the Soviet country-wide air-defense system had been designed not against missiles but against bombers, and that construction of the ABM system around Moscow has been halted halfway. In spite of that, the MIRV program was continued — justified by the new argument that we had to be able to destroy a larger number of targets in the U.S.S.R. It didn't take great expertise to understand that deploying these *MIRV's* could destabilize the state of mutual deterrence: With each MIRV'ed missile capable of destroying more than one missile silo, a surprise pre-emptive strike aimed at destroying the other side's entire land-based missile force would become a worrisome possibility. Yet little heed was paid to this aspect of the program.

It stood to reason that the Soviet Union would match our MIRV program with one of its own. Yet when the strategic arms limitation talks (SALT) began in 1969, the Pentagon vetoed suggestions that the United States propose a moratorium on MIRV development by both sides. At that juncture, such a freeze could have been accomplished by simple agreement, with little likelihood of undetectable violations. Today, with MIRV's being extensively deployed within the Soviet Union, detection is a much more difficult problem, and concern about this new factor is understandably acute in the United States. Once again, a missed opportunity for restraint has led to another erosion in our security.

The same blind opposition to restraint in American weapons development has plagued every effort to arrive at a total nuclear-test ban. Opponents of the idea in the 50's and 60's concocted elaborate scenarios on the feasibility of clandestine Soviet tests, befogging the central issue that a comprehensive ban would have been to our advantage, in view of our technological lead. Once again, the political opposition prevailed: the Kennedy Administration *had to settle for a partial ban,* limited to tests in the atmosphere, in outer space and under water. The treaty, concluded in 1963, is now adhered to by many nations, though not, among the nuclear powers, by France and China. It has resulted in an immense reduction in radioactive fallout from nuclear testing above ground. But underground testing has been pushed by the superpowers at a much faster clip, so that development of new nuclear weapons has continued as before.

## A Significant Accomplishment

The SALT I agreement signed by President Nixon and Secretary General Brezhnev in Moscow in 1972 was accompanied by much fanfare about detente that has been rendered questionable by the passage of time. Yet the atmospherics were accompanied by a significant accomplishment — a treaty to limit each side to only two ABM sites (later reduced to one); to refrain from testing and deploying new ABM technology; and, most important, to refrain from interfering with each other's technical means, such as satellites, of gathering intelligence on each other's weapons development.

The American and Soviet Governments' willingness to virtually strip their territories of ABM defenses made the population of each of the two countries hostage, in effect, to the other's strategic nuclear force. By inference, the treaty recognized that a surprise attack by either side would be too wildly irrational for any sane Government to undertake. Under the conditions that prevailed in 1972, no surprise attack could be expected to destroy the other side's offensive forces; most of those forces would be left undamaged — far more than enough to inflict lethal destruction on the aggressor nation's populace and civilization. In such a war, there could be no winner.

SALT I also produced a five-year interim agreement on offensive missiles. This left our strategic forces unchanged, while putting a ceiling on further expansion of Soviet land-based missiles — but, in recognition of the Soviets' weaker overall position, permitting further numerical expansion of their sea-based missile force. Today, the forces on both sides stand at about the agreed level — some 1,400 Soviet versus 1,054 American land-based ICBM's, and about 900 Soviet versus 656 American submarine-based ballistic missiles. To these should be added more than 400 American heavy bombers, armed with air-to-ground missiles or gravity bombs, versus 140 rather obsolescent Soviet bombers. The Soviet Union now has about a two-to-one advantage in megatonnage — the total nuclear payload or "throw weight" of its missile forces. But the United States, because of its more extensive MIRV-ing, has about 7,500 missile warheads, smaller but much more accurate than the Soviet Union's 3,900. This gives the United States a two-to-one advantage in targeted warheads — the truest measure of nuclear strength — quite apart from our superiority in bombers.

There the situation remains, except for the refinements added by President Ford and Secretary Brezhnev at their 1974 meeting in Vladivostok. The guidelines produced there — never converted to a formal agreement — set a top limit of 2,400 offensive delivery vehicles (whether strategic missiles or bombers) for each side, with the qualification that only 1,320 of these could be MIRV'ed. Our forces today are well below this total, but not much below the MIRV-ing limit; the Soviet Union's forces are slightly over the total numerically but nowhere near the permitted quota for MIRV's. The destructive potential on each side is staggering — at least a thousand times greater than that of all the bombs exploded during World War II.

In this history of the nuclear arms race, the United States has been first with most of the technological innovations and new weapons systems, except for some systems of defense, to which the Soviet Union has traditionally dedicated a far greater portion of its military effort. The American innovations — such as heavy bombers, solid-fueled missiles (whether land-based or aboard submarines), inertial guidance and MIRV's — were all followed a few years later by the Soviet versions. Soviet political and military writers have argued that the nuclear arms race is in large measure a consequence of this pattern of American innovation — and, hence, solely the fault of the United States. The truth is not that simple.

Soviet military intelligence analysts, reading transcripts of Congressional committee hearings, the budgets and annual "posture statements" of the Secretary of Defense, periodicals like Aviation Week and other open material, have no trouble obtaining fairly accurate knowledge of American forces in being and of what they will be like a few years hence. For us, however, reliable estimates of current Soviet military capabilities were virtually unobtainable a couple of decades ago, and only the advent of sophisticated "national technical means" of information gathering, such as satellites, has rectified this deficiency to some degree. Projection of future Soviet capabilities, however, still depends largely on value judgments, in view of the lack of open public debate on these matters in the Soviet Union, and in view of the Soviet practice of shrouding official policy statements in generalities. By necessity, therefore, American projections, such as the National Intelligence Estimates, involve a wide range of possibilities. The "worst-case" assessment that frequently prevails can often call for anticipatory measures, including a research-and-development project for some novel weapon system. This prudent, if often exaggerated, American reaction has not differed, in essence, from the ways other nations have responded to similar stimuli. It is something the Soviet leaders would have been wise to foresee, since prodding the American military industry into greater production cannot have been part of their objective, and is clearly against their interests, as it is against ours.

On several occasions, as we have noted, American proponents of an uncompromising "worst-case" view of Soviet intentions have sought to swing public opinion behind them. Sometimes their efforts have taken the form of exaggerated stories devoid of technical foundation — current science fiction about particle-beam weapons are an example of the genre — that tend to spread concern. That, in turn, tends to generate additional pressures for a new American arms program to meet the new alleged threat. A heated campaign of this type has now been under way for about a year, led by two private groups — the newly formed Committee on the Present Danger and the older American Security Council (not to be confused with the National Security Council, the President's advisory body).

## The Views of the Hard-liners

The campaign was highlighted last December by leaks to the press about a collision between the professional group responsible for the National Intelligence Estimate and what the reports described as the winner of the contest — an ad-hoc "Team B" of outsiders selected by the Ford White House to represent the "hard line" view. "Team B" concluded, to no one's surprise, that there was an imminent threat of Soviet domination of the world. Its findings are said to have been largely dismissed by the Carter Administration, after a detailed study, but the thrust provided by the episode is still very much with us. The views of the hardliners deserve our careful consideration.

While some members of this school have made much of a possible gap between Soviet and American capabilities, it is Soviet *intentions* that have dominated the new debate, almost to the exclusion of technical realities. Those who have sounded the alarm anew are fond of citing Soviet military writers to show that the Soviets reject the concept of mutual deterrence, stress the Clausewitz dictum that war is but an extension of diplomacy, and deny that nuclear weapons have ruled out war as a policy option. For instance, it is pointed out, in his 1963 book on military strategy, Soviet Marshal Vassily Sokolovsky argued that nuclear war can be fought and won by the Soviet Union.

Citing Soviet military writers as guides to Soviet Union's policy is, however, of questionable value. The argument attributed to Sokolovsky has been developed by other Soviet officers as well, but what should one expect from a senior Soviet military figure? Should he tell his juniors that they cannot win a future nuclear war? In the old Stalinist days he would have been stood up against the wall and shot for such heresy.

Even if genuine, belief that nuclear wars can be "won" is not limited to Soviet generals and marshals. Gen. Curtis LeMay, of Strategic Air Command fame, used to urge on us an ability "to fight and win any war — including a general war." Former Defense Secretary Melvin Laird, in his book "A House Divided" (issued in 1962 and reissued in 1969), wrote that our "strategy must aim at fighting, winning and recovering"; that we must therefore develop "the willingness . . . to wage total nuclear war," and that we must make it "credible to the enemy that we will take the initiative and strike first." Another Defense Secretary of the Nixon era, James Schlesinger, talked repeatedly while in office of "surgical" strikes against military targets, and of other aspects of waging "flexible" nuclear wars.

The plain fact is that it is easy to find examples of aggressive or provocative utterances on both sides. But it is definitely not a fact that they represent the stated policies or known beliefs of the leaders of either country. In any case, statements of political intent, unsupported by capability, should be pretty much discounted. The real question is whether the Soviet Union could arrive at the military capability to bring the United States to its knees.

The hard-line scenario for such an eventuality goes something like this:

By the time it completes deploying its very heavy — and now MIRV'ed — SS-18 ICBM and its somewhat smaller SS-19, the Soviet Union will have the capability to destroy virtually all American ICBM's in their silos, all our bombers not in flight, and all our missile submarines in port — all this at one blow and with the expenditure of only a small part of its missile forces. A massive Soviet civil-defense program, now under way, will provide blast shelters for the country's political and industrial cadres, while the plain people will be told to evacuate the cities and dig fallout shelters for themselves in the countryside — a process, according to Soviet civil-defense manuals, that is to take three days. Since the only remaining American forces would be those armed with small warheads, Soviet cities and industrial plants could be restored within an acceptable period of time after an American retaliatory strike; and, because of the mass-evacuation measures, there would be only 10 million to 20 million Soviet citizens killed — no more than perished during World War II. By contrast, the remaining Soviet strategic forces could destroy American society totally, and kill a large part of the population. Confronted with such a prospect, the United States would concede world hegemony to the Soviet Union without war.

## The Prophets' Past Record

How is one to evaluate this kind of thinking? What, for one thing, is the past record of the prophets? Many of the men who proclaimed the bomber gap, the missile gap and the ABM gap are the very ones who today warn of the civil-defense gap and the Soviet Union's nuclear superiority. Paul Nitze, for example, was chairman of the staff that produced N.S.C. 68 in 1950 and a member of the Gaither panel in 1957. During the missile buildup, the test-ban debates and the ABM scares of the 60's, he was Secretary of the Navy and Deputy Secretary of Defense. He was a member of the "Team B" in 1976, and is one of the moving spirits of the Committee on the Present Danger.

Men of Nitze's persuasion are entitled, of course, to their opinion, and no one should question their motives or their good faith. But the American public, in evaluating that opinion, may well ask whether it is a reflection of reality or a repetition of the all too familiar myth-making of the past.

It is difficult to regard these doomsday scenarios as anything more than baseless nightmares. First, an attack on our very hard — that is, blast -and shock-resistant — missile silos would be a highly complex and very uncertain operation. The first nuclear explosions of the first incoming warheads can destroy the other warheads still flying into the target area, and they can do so in ways and for periods of time that cannot be calculated accurately in advance. Some of the targeted missile silos would thus be left undestroyed, and the attacker would have to cope with an unpredictable number of retaliatory ICBM's launched during and after his strike.

Nor would it be a simple matter for the Soviets to catch us off our guard with a surprise attack. We would in all likelihood have advance warnings of less obvious nature than the trek of millions of Muscovites armed with shovels to the countryside. Our space sensors would be primed to signal a Soviet launch; or they would be put out of commission in advance by Soviet antisatellite systems, and this in itself would alert us to imminent attack. The Soviets well know that, instead of waiting a minute longer, the

American President could order our own ICBM's launched against the Soviet Union, leaving empty silos for the Soviets to destroy.

Moreover, an American retaliatory strike by only a portion of our strategic force would inflict damage of such magnitude that the ability of Soviet society to recover from the blow would be in serious question. By the mid-80's, our Polaris, Poseidon and Trident submarines — two-thirds of them safely at sea at all times — will be armed with about 7,000 missile warheads. The smallest of these warheads will have at least three to four times the explosive power of the Hiroshima bomb. The Soviet Union has a fragile transportation system, mostly railroads and ship canals; its heavy industries tend to be concentrated in giant units; its cities are compact. Our submarine-based warheads alone could wreak total destruction on nearly all Soviet habitation centers, industrial plants, railroad yards, canal locks and airfields.

## The Spectre of Soviet Civil Defense

As to the latest evocation of the specter of Soviet civil defense, this rests on gross exaggeration of the program's ability to protect the populace. It is asserted that the Soviets spend five to 10 times more on civil defense that we spend in the United States, and it is true that their manuals imply a state of great preparedness, including plans for the evacuation of their cities. But American civil-defense manuals similarly claim a state of readiness that includes shelters for nearly the entire population; the literature goes into descriptions of blast shelters for millions in mine galleries. Yet it requires only a short sojourn in our cities to realize that the populace, except for the civil defense officialdom, is so uninvolved in these preparations that it would take a long and arduous effort by the American Government to put the country on a state of civilian preparedness.

Common sense suggests that the Soviet civil-defense program is not unlike our own. But let us, for the sake of argument, accept the claims that our hard-liners make on its behalf. How effective, even then, could the program be? The Soviet populace and the more privileged cadres, on emerging from their shelters shortly after an American strike, would find themselves without transportation; facing starvation; without shelter for the winter in a landscape of ruined cities and towns contaminated by radioactivity and millions of decaying bodies; with tens of millions of victims of radiation sickness to care for, and with epidemics certainly in store.

What rational policymaker would take action inviting consequences of that sort? Our "realists" nonetheless insist that the Soviet Government can be expected to do just that — and to use arms-control agreements as subterfuge for advancing toward global hegemony. What they propose is that we proceed to arm ourselves at an accelerated pace, so as to put the United States in a position of military superiority beyond the Soviets' reach. What awaits us if we succumb to this advice and, in the words of one of the proponents of that course, "arms ourselves to the teeth"?

Some of our actions are likely to be potentially provocative. Thus, by equipping our Minuteman III with the new Mk 12A warheads, and with the ultraprecise guidance systems that are now in an advanced state of development, we would make that missile into an effective weapon against the Soviets' land-based ICBM's, the backbone of their strategic forces. If we then proceed to deploy our MX ICBM — a larger follow-up on the Minuteman that is now under development — it would increase the explosive potential of our offensive force still further. If the MX missiles are made mobile, instead of being stationary, as our silo-based missiles are at present, the Soviets will be left in the dark about the very magnitude of our ICBM forces.

## The Cruise Missile

President Carter's decision to deploy the long-range cruise missile, designed to be launched from B-52 bombers some distance from Soviet borders, may be compatible with the mutual-deterrence posture, if kept within the authorized limits. But deploying a much larger number of cruise missiles with long-range capacity — missiles that could be launched from land or sea from just about all points of the compass — would totally negate the mutual monitoring of strategic forces now in effect and could be regarded as highly provocative by the Soviet Union.

The Soviets, of course, will not be indifferent to such moves; we can be sure that, once again, they will respond in kind. Deployment of the MIRV'ed SS-18, and of the still more advanced missiles that, according to Defense Secretary Harold Brown, are now under development, will doubtless be stepped up. Mobile ICBM systems can be expected to spread over the land mass of the Soviet Union, leaving us in reciprocal ignorance about the number of missiles deployed. After a few years' time, we will learn of the deployment of the Soviet version of our long-range cruise missiles — perhaps aboard ships off our coats.

In this atmosphere of all-out competition for military superiority, any political crisis that may arise between the United States and the Soviet Union is not likely to be resolved the way the Cuban missile crisis was in 1962. That experience must have been a humiliating one not only for Khrushchev but for the entire Soviet hierarchy. Since then, the Soviets have made major sacrifices for their huge armament effort, designed to assure that never again will they have to back down on a major issue because of military inferiority to the United States. The American people, for their part, have had much difficulty in accepting the Soviet Union as equal to the United States in power terms on the international plane. To give in to the Soviet Union in some future crisis might be infinitely difficult for us. Because of these attitudes both in Washington and in Moscow, the crisis could become unmanageable, in spite of the hot line and the Soviet-American agreement of 1973 not to seek recourse to nuclear arms.

Apart from the risk of war by miscalculation, due to the hair-trigger readiness of the strategic forces of both sides, there are other factors that will make crisis situations increasingly probable if the strategic arms race is allowed to heat up. For example, increased emphasis on nuclear arms by the superpowers would intensify the urge among non-nuclear states to acquire nuclear weapons. That would create new focuses for the germination of nuclear wars. In that new context, Soviet-American cooperation on measures against nuclear proliferation is likely to collapse. And without such East-West cooperation — evidenced recently by the intense pressure on South Africa to suspend preparations for a nuclear weapons test — nuclear proliferation around the world is certain to accelerate.

Another adverse effect would arise in the area of "conventional" arms. The strategic arms race has been paralleled by an arms race for general armed forces, including tactical (or battlefield) nuclear warheads and all types of conventional arms. Advanced conventional weapons and delivery systems have become a substantial part of international trade. Some of the hardware being provided to the non-nuclear countries could be used to deliver nuclear warheads, and this makes acquisition of a nuclear capability more tempting to those states.

Imported modern arms have been used in numerous local wars since the end of World War II. Through the sale of such arms, the superpowers have acquired a patron status in many of these regions — this apart from local conflicts in which the superpowers' involvement was more direct. If the arms race heats up, the patron-client relationship characteristic of the third world will inevitably be emphasized, and the occasion for Soviet-American confrontations, like the one that occurred during the 1973 Mideast war, will be multiplied.

## The Priorities for Arms Control

Is all this inevitable? Yes, but only if we fail to make a genuine effort to end or at least curb the Soviet-American arms race and progress toward a more satisfactory state of detente, or peaceful coexistence, than we now have. There are, of course, risks inherent in the effort — though far smaller than the risks of an intensified nuclear arms race — and we should be clear-eyed in making the attempt. We should, for example, assure ourselves of adequate means to verify Soviet compliance with any agreements we reach. But to reach such agreements, we must — unequivocally — concede equal status to the Soviet Union and accept its own legitimate security needs.

The ultimate objective should be the elimination of all nuclear arsenals. But more immediately urgent is the need to stop deploying those new strategic weapon systems that destabilize deterrence and increase tensions by virtue of their provocative character. Top priority should go to an agreement to curtail further deployment of any "counterforce" missiles (those aimed against the other side's missile silos) that have already been developed. A close second should be an agreement to limit missile tests to those necessary for the quality control of deployments already in effect. Both agreements could be monitored by currently accepted, nonintrusive means of vertification. Each would go far toward stabilizing the state of mutual deterrence.

High priority should also go to an international treaty for a total nuclear test ban. A move in that direction would signify to the rest of the world that the superpowers are in earnest about ending the nuclear arms race. Constraints against nuclear proliferation would be immeasurably strengthened if the ban covered not only weapons tests but so-called peaceful nuclear explosions — a proposition seemingly agreed to by Brezhnev in a recent speech.

Progress along this road would be rocky, at best, because of the different natures of American and Soviet societies, because of mutual suspicions nurtured by many years of angry confrontation, and because of the opposition of the hard-liners in both camps. President Carter's SALT proposals of last March constituted an important move toward genuine arms control, and it is regrettable that they were summarily rejected by the Soviet Union. Progress, or lack of it, in the current SALT II negotiations will indicate whether the proposals were rejected because they were sprung on the Soviets, as some say; or because some of the specifics were disadvantageous to the Soviets, as Moscow claimed; or because of an intrinsically hard-line position of the Soviet Union, as our own hard-liners assert. One must hope that the initial Soviet reaction is not the final one, that a SALT II agreement will be reached, and that this will be the starting point for a winding down of the arms race and a new and safer era.

# SALT AND BEYOND —
# POSSIBILITIES AND PROSPECTS
## By Sidney D. Drell

As a new Administration and Congress take office, the United States has an especially opportune moment and need to review our present strategic nuclear deterrent. In addition to reviewing the sufficiency of our existing military forces, we must now also assess the adequacy of our planned forces to meet the needs of stable deterrence, since today's programs will provide the force structure on which our national security will rely beyond 1984.

The country faces imminent decisions on whether or at what rate to pursue weapons programs designed to maintain, modernize and improve each component of our strategic nuclear deterrent force of missiles and long-range bombers. These important decisions, which will determine the character, strength, and possible missions of our strategic nuclear forces in the late 1980s, depend on many factors: our national policy goals; the missions of our strategic forces in support of these goals; Soviet actions and emerging threats; arms control implications; and dollar costs. Essentially, there are two kinds of questions we must answer in making these decisions: the *need for* and the *arms control impact of* the weapon programs under consideration. For example:

B-1 Bomber and Trident submarine. The determining factor in the decisions on these two programs is cost versus effectivness. Do we need their improved capabilities and are they worth their great expense, or are there more cost-effective alternatives for modernizing our forces?

With regard to programs to improve missile accuracy and to increase warhead yields, in particular the new M-X mobile land-based missile, the new Mk-12a ICBM warhead, and the MaRV (maneuverable reentry vehicle), the determining factor is their future implication for arms con-

*Sidney Drell is Professor and Deputy Director of the Stanford Linear Accelerator Center. His presentation here is based on an article in the Bulletin of the Atomic Scientists, May, 1977, which combined papers presented earlier to the Senate Foreign Relations Committee and the Civilian/Military Institute National Symposium at the U.S. Air Force Academy.*

trol and strategic stability. Will they harm or help prospects for maintaining a stable strategic balance, preferably at lower levels of weaponry?

Cruise missile. Both questions of need and arms control impact are of comparable import in the decisions about the long-range strategic cruise missile.

At the outset let me state my perception of today's strategic balance.

I believe that the strategic forces of the United States are immensely powerful. The Soviet Union has no edge, let alone advantage, in their overall strategic forces. Claims to the contrary, such as the allegation that the Soviets have achieved a strategic superiority and that we have lost an effective retaliatory capability, are not and cannot be supported by facts.

In some specific instances, however, such as the size of the Soviet fixed land-based intercontinental ballistic missiles and their total explosive power, or the megatonnage which these missiles can deliver, the Soviets do hold a lead as a result of design choices made by them as well as by the United States. However, as far as reliability, accuracy, number of warheads, and advanced technology, our lead is impressive.

## U.S. Forces More Than Adequate

I believe that our strategic nuclear forces are at present far more than adequate to fulfill their single vital mission of deterrence of nuclear attack. The Soviet Union, or any other potential nuclear foe, knows that whatever the attack, we *can* retaliate; and that it is our stated *intention* to retaliate in a manner commensurate with the provocation, even if it means destroying a substantial portion of their society. This is "assured destruction."

Essentially all responsible analysts agree with this assessment of the *present* robust state of our strategic nuclear deterrent and recognize its adequacy for meeting current policy goals. However, there are seriously and substantially divergent projections as to where we will find ourselves in the *future* if current trends are projected ahead to 1984 and beyond. Irrespective of these ambiguities, the issue we face as a nation is to determine the actions required *now* with respect both to weapons and arms control initiatives in order to preserve our national security in the coming decade.

In singling out deterrence of nuclear attack among the missions of our strategic nuclear forces, I am emphasizing that there are no sensible alternatives to a policy of deterrence for the foreseeable future. Other missions for our strategic nuclear forces have frequently been proposed, ranging from political or military coercion to limited nuclear war fighting and "winning." However, you can't win if you don't survive.

I am convinced that the overwhelmingly likely course of events of actually implementing these options is an escalation of hostilities to almost total, mutual destruction. Hence, I conclude that deterrence of nuclear attack is the proper mission of our nuclear forces. Weapons development and force structures must be planned toward this goal as the single overriding priority.

## Criteria for Arms Control Policy

The requirement of having an "assured destruction" capability to devastate any nation which has initiated a nuclear attack even against our own retaliatory forces is fundamental to deterrence. Above and beyond this, however, a policy of *stable* deterrence between the United States and the Soviet Union has six important components, which should be the determining criteria in our decision on the evolution of strategic weapons and on arms control policy.

1. *Clear evidence that neither country seeks strategic superiority.*

We face an ever-upward spiraling arms race of deployments and counter-deployments unless both countries understand the folly and futility of striving for superiority of their strategic nuclear forces. Both countries have officially renounced the quest for superiority, but their programs and forces must be perceived as being compatible with stated policy. The ABM treaty of 1972 at SALT I represents an important achievement in this regard.

2. *A rough overall equivalence of strategic forces.*

This requirement is important to us since we must convince our people and our allies as well as the Soviet Union that our commitment to deterrence is firm and genuine. However, an insistence on strict equality in each individual measure of the strategic forces of both nations would serve no useful purpose for deterrence and would effectively block prospects for effective arms control.

It is particularly destructive to insist on equality in selective categories of weapons in which one perceives the opponents to be superior, but to ignore or minimize those in which one's own forces are superior. The forces of the United States and the Soviet Union have evolved in different technological styles and are embedded in different bureaucratic structures as well as geographical and political conditions. Independent of their differences in numbers of warheads, size of missiles, or reliance on manned bombers, they are in rough overall balance. Both are capable of inconceivably enormous devastation, even after absorbing a first strike from the opponent.

3. *A mix of strategic forces designed so that a large fraction of each will survive a preemptive attack.*

The existence of major strategic forces of either nation that are recognized as highly vulnerable to attack is a cause for concern to both the beholder and the possessor. The possessor would undoubtedly feel threatened by prospects of a preemptive first strike and the beholder of a major force of vulnerable weapons would surely be concerned that the only reason for their existence would be in a first-strike role. Such a force would appear to be particularly ominous in a time of heightened tension by the requirement that it be launched on warning before being destroyed itself.

The current U.S. national security debate indicates that there is widespread concern, as there should be if deployments continue, about the possibility that our fixed land-based Minutemen might become vulnerable to potential Soviet threats. To be sure, the missile submarines at sea and the alert strategic bombers are not subject to destruction in a preemptive attack. However, if we are to maintain the present stable strategic environment there should be neither a real nor a "plausibly perceived" vulnerability of any major component of the strategic deterrent forces on either side. We are all much better off without such vulnerabilities since deterrence can be preserved by other means.

4. *Secure and effective command and control of one's nuclear forces.*

Secure, invulnerable, and effective command and control links are crucial in war and in peace. Under nuclear attack they must survive if we are to retain confidence in our retaliatory capability and in our control of the nature and the extent of that retaliation. In peace they must provide effective protection against unauthorized or accidental nuclear launch.

5. *Maintenance of strong conventional non-nuclear military forces.*

The maintenance of strong conventional forces is important if we are to have effective non-nuclear military options for meeting our national security goals and commitments. In the event of local or theater combat, the United States must be prepared to meet the threat and stabilize the conflict short of crossing the one-way bridge from non-nuclear to nuclear warfare.

Strong and effective conventional military forces can increase the time for serious political efforts to resolve a limited conflict before the military situation takes a decisive turn and "gets out of hand." Once that happens, there will be the severe temptation and risk of crossing the nuclear threshold. Greater emphasis must be given to toughening and modernizing these conventional forces. They are our balance to the growing Soviet ability to project their power outwards from their borders and away from their shores.

6. *The existence of "flexible" response alternatives to "massive retaliation."*

It has long been recognized in defining the requirements of deterrence that nuclear weapons might be launched with less than maximum force by either side. This requirement of "flexible response" can be implemented by our present forces. In fact, the flexibility of our strategic forces was greatly enhanced by the ABM Treaty of SALT I. As a result of that treaty, the large number of warheads deployed in our MIRVed missiles, primarily to penetrate postulated Soviet ABM systems, need no longer be assumed to be attrited by Soviet defenses. With our extensive and recently modernized retargeting capabilities the President presently has many alternatives to the intentional and almost certainly suicidal attack on civilian populations.

Of course, the potential benefits of any limited nuclear action by the United States must be weighed against the clear risk that the Soviet response would itself not be limited. In this regard, there is no evidence of Soviet developments of low-yield weapons designed to minimize civilian casualties. Hence, it is hard to be sanguine about prospects for limiting the casualties to the U.S. population by actually implementing such "limited response" options. Nevertheless it may be argued that this capability enhances deterrence on psychological and political grounds by greatly increasing our military options, although our chances of survival after initial nuclear use may not be improved substantially.

Flexible response, if extended too broadly, however, can create serious difficulties for stable deterrence. These will arise when the requirements of flexible response are extended to include "hard-target counterforce" and when the deployed forces are technically capable of implementing it. "Hard-target counterforce" refers to the ability to strike hardened military targets, such as the underground ICBM silos, efficiently and selectively and to destroy them with high confidence.

## The Schlesinger Doctrine

During the past three years this shift in emphasis of flexible response to include hard-target counterforce has received considerable attention in this country; it is frequently referred to as the "Schlesinger doctrine" since the former Defense Secretary has been its most notable spokesman. If adopted as policy, the Schlesinger doctrine is cited to require two major new U.S. defense programs. One is the development and deployment of improved and modernized ICBMs capable of destroying Soviet missile silos with high confidence. The other is a major expansion of the civil defense program, which has been only moderately active since the early 1960s. The Schlesinger doctrine justifies civil defense as necessary to improve the credibility of our limited nuclear war posture by evacuating, relocating, and protecting the civilian population from the effects of limited Soviet nuclear attacks.

By giving added emphasis to preparations for fighting and "winning" limited nuclear wars aimed at one another's strategic arsenals, the Schlesinger doctrine threatens to undermine the stability of the strategic balance.

The deployment of weapons designed and developed to destroy hardened ICBMs conflicts directly with condition (3) for maintaining stable deterrence. Extensive civil defense exercises, along with the deployment of such weapons, will inevitably be interpreted by a potential foe as preparations to threaten, if not actually launch, a first-nuclear strike. Moreover, if this policy were implemented by the United States, the widespread diffusion throughout the population of the required civil defense activities and preparations would raise profound questions of basic values and priorities of our society.

No valid military justification has been advanced to support an extension of the existing broad range of flexible response options to include hard-target counterforce. Orginally it was claimed that with extensive civil defense available we "could reduce nationwide fatalities due to fallout from a limited Soviet counterforce attack to relatively low levels — well under 1 million." This led to the conclusion that "the likelihood of limited nuclear attacks cannot be challenged on the assumption that massive civilian fatalities and injuries would result," and that therefore we were obliged to prepare for such conflict.

However, subsequent detailed analyses by the Department of Defense and by the Congressional Office of Technology Assessment, in response to questions raised by members of the Senate Foreign Relations Committee, showed these figures and claims to be misleading. These analyses indicated in fact that those counterforce strikes launched against the United States which actually caused relatively few civilian casualties would be strategically insignificant; and that strikes inflicting appreciable damage to U.S. strategic forces would cause very large civilian fatalities, numbering at least 10 to 20 million, due to fallout, even if it is assumed that the population made extensive use of civil defense protection.

In all cases the United States was left with such a massive retaliatory capability as to make the counterforce strategy appear to be ineffective from the Soviet point of view. In addition, there is no assurance that once nuclear weapons are launched against military targets the subsequent conflict will be limited to them.

We currently have a very broad and fully adequate repertoire of flexible response options against many military targets. Their further extension to include hard-target counterforce would be dangerous to strategic stability and should be rejected.

## Strategic Program Trends

Since the SALT I agreements were signed in May 1972 the United States and the Soviet Union have continued their strategic weapons developments. The overall scope and intensity of Soviet military programs, their civil defense efforts and, particularly, their initiation of MIRVing their new land-based missiles — these developments are viewed with disappointment by some and with suspicion, if not outright alarm, by others.

The Soviets publicly endorse the principle of maintaining an overall strategic balance rather than striving for superiority, and there is as yet no persuasive evidence that their deeds belie their words. Yet what must concern us is the actual effect of their persistent military buildup. How does it affect our ability to meet all the criteria for strategic stability that I have just described? How should we respond to these disturbing indicators with new weapons programs?

Since the conclusion of the SALT I agreement the Soviets have also had cause of concern about U.S. programs, for we too have MIRVed very extensively and have also substantially improved missile accuracy. Our development and test programs have had neither the intensity nor scope of the Soviet missile programs, and our considerably smaller missiles and warheads appear less ominous as a hard-target counterforce threat than do the Soviet missiles.

Nevertheless, the United States with its lead in technology, presently has many more deployed MIRVs. And the United States is pursuing highly sophisticated accuracy programs that are frequently justified in terms of their potential for destroying hardened ICBM silos. Thus, it is not without cause that the Soviet Union, with far more of its retaliatory power in its fixed land-based ICBMs than we have in ours, shows concern with our programs similar to our concern with theirs.

In this atmosphere of mutually aggravated perceptions, prospects for arms control remedies have dimmed. However, neither side has as yet extensively deployed missiles designed and capable as hard-target killers, and a *strategic balance exists today*. With appropriate mutual restraint the United States and the Soviet Union can maintain the criteria for stable deterrence that I described above.

The new Soviet land-based MIRVs and their civil defense activities are the two programs that have caused greatest concern and triggered claims by some that the Soviets are intending to attain "strategic superiority." I will analyze the status of these activities in turn, describing the issues they raise for our national security and what I believe to be the appropriate U.S. response.

## New Soviet MIRVs

The new Soviet MIRVs (the SS-17, SS-18, and SS-19) have the throw-weight and potentially both the accuracy and reliability, if their observed high rate of missile test firings continues, to pose a hard-target counterforce threat against our ICBMs. If their current buildup continues and grows into a potential threat to our full ICBM force, a response by the United States will be required in order to fulfill condition (3) for survivable forces.* It is widely recognized that there are enormous technical dif-

---

*Some have alleged that continued MIRV deployments by the Soviets will also deny condition (2), the rough overall balance of strategic forces. I disagree with this analysis, which greatly overemphasizes missile throw-weight as an overall strategic indicator relative to other factors such as accuracy, reliability and the number of warheads, in all of which the United States holds the edge. As Jan Lodal pointed out in the April, 1976 *Foreign Affairs*, "total megatonnage is simply not a very accurate measure, or even a very meaningful measure, of strategic force capability." Lodal also comments that "there is only a very narrow range of accuracies in which throw-weight is important to a hard-target counterforce capability." In any event, when total missile throw-weight and gross bomber payloads are added up, there is no projected Soviet throw-weight advantage in the decade ahead.

ficulties and uncertainties in mounting a coordinated attack designed to destroy a large fraction of these ICBMs (often mentioned in this regard is the fraticide problem). Nevertheless, just the remote risk that such an attack will succeed is likely to impel us to initiate remedial actions.

This issue can be met by the United States in various ways that involve new military systems or plans, but not without posing new difficulties as a result of the solution. Or, as discussed below, it can be resolved by major new arms control initiatives, such as an agreement to limit the modernization of missiles as well as the number of missile test firings. Such steps would effectively throttle the specific advances in weapons technology leading to hard-target counterforce capabilities.

First, I will consider four possible steps or options which have been suggested that the United States can take in order to resolve this issue by modifying our military forces or plans.

● *Replace fixed land-based ICBMs by "going to sea" with more sea-launched ballistic missiles (SLBMs).*

Were we to adopt this option, we would be abandoning the missile force with the most secure command and control as well as the most responsible operational flexibility. A much larger fraction of our deterrent would also be more sensitive to possible future ASW (antisubmarine warfare) breakthroughs. This option would, furthermore, be exceptionally expensive.

● *Replace fixed ICBMs by mobile land-based or shelter-based ICBMs.*

The verification problems raised by this option could mean the end of arms control by negotiated agreements. A deceptively based system which shuttles missiles between many different shelters, or possible launch points, could lead to many thousands of shelters throughout the Soviet Union and completely negate the SALT process which is based on counting *missile launchers.* It violates the SALT I provisions unless each individual shelter, whether or not occupied by a missile, is counted as a launcher. If, on the other hand, each shelter is counted, this concept is meaningless unless their allowed number greatly exceeds the numerical limits agreed to at SALT I or Vladivostok.

All analyses show that mobile missiles not deceptively based are of advantage to the Soviet Union because of their much larger land areas available for deploying such systems. In the open U.S. society, mobile missiles would be confined to the western deserts under conditions that would make them vulnerable to barrage. Therefore closing off this area of potential arms competition, which also poses verification difficulties, is in the U.S. interest.

● *Modify SALT I so as to permit deployment of an ABM system designed solely for defending small hardened military targets such as ICBM missile silos and launch control facilities.*

The option would force us to modify, if not abandon, the most successful treaty achieved at SALT thus far, that is, the limit on ABM deployments to one site only. Furthermore, it is not at all clear that it is physically feasible to design an ABM system that is effective for defending missile silos and at the same time has no significant potential for upgrading to a nationwide area defense.

• *Retain and further harden the ICBMs and adopt a "launch on warning" doctrine with or without arming or disarming signals.*

The option to "launch on warning" would make the world a much more dangerous place to live in during time of tension due to either potential accidents or failure of communications.

All of these options, if adopted singly or in combination, create their own serious new problems. Thus, I recommend against all four of the above options, in favor of an effective and available arms control option to limit the number of missile test firings, as I will propose below.

## Absurdity of Civil Defense

Recently we have been hearing about Soviet civil defense measures and their purported threat to U.S. security. In particular, T. K. Jones, whose calculations are frequently referred to when such claims are made in this connection, concluded in Congressional testimony that "The Soviet civil defense preparations substantially undermine the deterrence concept that has been the cornerstone of U.S. national security."

I totally disagree with this conclusion. I know of no intelligence information or technical facts on which to base a conclusion that Soviet civil defense programs are effective to the point of denying the U.S. retaliatory capability or even of threatening to disturb significantly the overall U.S. and Soviet strategic balance.

We have been learning more about Soviet civil defense activities as a result of paying considerably more attention to them. We are finding them to be more extensive than some had previously believed, although traditionally the Soviets have devoted a larger portion of their military budget to defenses, including an extensive air defense system which the United States wisely has chosen not to match. But I know of no evidence of a crash civil defense effort nor of their achieving an effective defense of either the population or the industrial base.

A confident estimate of the effectiveness of a nationwide civil defense system can never be given by either country, no matter how detailed the calculations and quantitative the claims, due to the enormity of the unknowns.

For a given megatonnage of attack the fatality levels due to fallout can change by many millions of lives depending on wind velocities and burst altitudes alone. For massive attacks the uncertainties are even greater in terms of the long-term ecological effects and the problems of reestablishing a society in the midst of devastation on an unparalleled scale.

The effectiveness of a civil defense system should also not be judged on the basis of survival manuals and guides. Both countries have created an extensive literature in this field. Recent reports by the U.S. Defense Civil Preparedness Agency list the identified U.S. shelter capacity as about 227 million persons. There are spaces for 90 percent of our population in the "Community Shelter Plan." Yet no one would claim that the U.S. program would prevent massive civilian casualties in the event of nuclear war. Evidently an effective operating civil defense system is not a matter of satistics and manuals.

In spite of these uncertainties we must nevertheless make our best judgments based on the facts available. The situation as I see it has been well summed up by Secretary of Defense Harold Brown.

Even if the Soviet Union is engaged in building up civilian shelters, Brown commented, there is little reason to believe that such a program would in fact confer a significant advantage in the event of a nuclear war. He then added: "The way to counter a relatively ineffective system is not to replicate it on the other side." And Brown concluded, "The belief on either side that you can survive a strategic thermonuclear war as a going society — when you can't — is the worst possible situation for the world to be in."

Why then do we hear the opposite conclusion, that Soviet civil defense preparations have undermined deterrence? Evidently it is necessary to scrutinize carefully the general assumptions that are made and the detailed factors that are ignored in any specific analysis and judge whether or not they are credible.

For example, in the analysis by T. K. Jones that I cited above, he concludes that survival from nuclear war is a matter of dispersal. Jones calculates that "a full 3-day evacuation of the type called for in Soviet plans would reduce their fatalities to no more than 10 million people."

I consider this conclusion to be absurd because of specific assumptions made in the analysis, as well as the factors ignored. However, before commenting on Jones' assumptions, I wish to emphasize my own belief that it is unproductive to dispute the precise level of expected civilian fatalities and detailed assumptions of civil protection. The underlying issue here is whether it is reasonable to presume that the Soviet Union would initiate a preemptive nuclear strike against the United States, if, on the basis of dubious assumptions, it calculated that our retaliatory blow would kill no more than 10 million civilians due to prompt effects of nuclear fallout alone in addition to destroying its cities and essentially all of its industrial base.

An irrational opponent who is undeterred from launching a nuclear first strike by the certain destruction of his society along with 10 million fatalities is hardly more likely to be deterred by prospects of a larger number of civilian fatalities, be it 30 or 50 or whatever million. In a world in which we are *mutual hostages* there is no defense against a MAD opponent who is willing to sacrifice destruction of his society and untold devastation. This observation in no way lessens the importance of the United States retaining the resolve as well as an adequate military strength to meet all the six requirements of stable deterrence that I discussed above.

Returning to Jones' statement and his description of the Soviet evacuation plans, we can assume that the United States would have at least three full days of intelligence available of ominous and imminent Soviet intentions as they evacuate their cities. Under these circumstances I can neither accept nor understand the assumption in his calculations that no more than one-half of our strategic arsenal would survive a Soviet first strike and be available for retaliation.

On the contrary, an appropriate U.S. response in the face of this clearly provocative Soviet action could be to put our entire retaliatory arsenal on the highest state of alert and to retarget the force in accordance with the pattern of evacuation. The President could announce, furthermore, that we are moving to a launch-on-warning policy for the duration of the provocation.

As a result of such actions, the United States could expect to have more than the normal fraction of our total retaliatory might available on target. The circumstances on which Jones based his calculations — assuming in particular the loss of about one-half of our entire land based force of 1,054 Minuteman and Titan ICBMs — could result only from a total failure of our civilian and military leadership.

Another crucial input into his calculations of "no more than 10 million" civilian fatalities is the special nature of the attacks and the extent of civilian protection he postulated. In one example the attack against a dispersed and unsheltered population was designed not to kill people: all weapons were air burst against industrial targets. In the other example he considered the opposite extreme: namely, an attack which was especially designed to produce fallout against the people. In this case, however, every man, woman, and child of the highly dispersed, evacuated population was assumed to be fully sheltered with a protection factor of 200.

The requirements to achieve such protection are awesome when translated into physical parameters: this level of protection means digging shelters in the evacuation region which provide a complete cover of more than two feet of solid dirt and which have a capacity to accommodate each and every person evacuated.

The Soviet civil defense manuals themselves estimate that a 12-man construction brigade must work for approximately 10 hours to prepare one such expedient shelter for 10 occupants. These shelters, moreover, in order to provide the claimed protection must be typically occupied around the clock, 24-hours-per day for at least a week and for most of the hours of each day for at least several more weeks thereafter. Moreover, water and food supplies must be prepared and available. What is not specified is how the Russians will achieve and sustain in practice such a comprehensive high level of protection. . . .

Moreover, the actual levels of casualties and fatalities in a major nuclear exchange doubtlessly will be much higher than indicated in naive calculations such as these that omit any estimates of all the disruptive effects that would occur in the immediate and long-range post-attack period. Recovery of a severely shocked society in the face of vast casualty levels, with food and water shortages, insufficient medical attention, with its major cities and industrial areas destroyed, and facing severe weather conditions is simply an unknown quantity. What we are talking about here is a far cry from the usual models of recovery in a localized disaster area surrounded by friendly, functioning communities.

I believe these uncertainties, in addition to the technically unjustified assumptions in analyses such as this, *totally invalidate claims that there exists a meaningful "civil defense gap" that threatens our deterrent.*

Perhaps the most worrisome aspect of Soviet civil defense activities is that they might lead their people and even their leaders to believe erroneously that they can really survive a nuclear conflict. Statements in this country enhancing that inaccurate view which ignores all human and physical realities increase that risk.

## Test-Firing Restraints

Both the United States and the Soviet Union could be effectively denied the possibility of developing a preemptive threat against each other's fixed land-based ICBMs by major new arms control initiatives.

The most promising of these would be an agreement to limit the number of missile test firings. Such a measure would be effective and can be adequately verified. An appropriate annual quota of roughly 10 to 20 missile test for each country would prevent attainment of those strategic objectives, in particular *confidence in success* of a preemptive first strike against land-based ICBMs, which have to rely on the demonstrated reliability and precision of complex systems. Such a limitation would be fully compatible with retaining confidence in the "assured destruction" role of our ICBM and SLBM missiles. This mission does not require such fine tuning of the system.

Balanced test-firing restraints will slow technology. This should help preserve the U.S. technological leadership since the same constraints are applied to both countries. What is proposed here is to constrain only the verifiable full-scale missile test and evaluation programs and not the un-verifiable R&D work which would continue as an important hedge against technological surprise or breakthrough.

There may be formidable difficulties in successfully negotiating such a treaty that effectively defers and limits new technology. Recall, however, that such a provision has already been successfully negotiated with respect to ABM systems in SALT I. With a missile test-firing restraint fixed land-based ICBMs would remain survivable. The need for new missile systems on grounds of survivability would be eliminated.

Balanced limitations on missile test firings by the United States and the Soviet Union would be a major step in arms control, furthering the goal to preserve the requirements of stable deterrence as described here. Furthermore, test-firing restraints will demonstrate to the world that the United States and the Soviet Union are honoring the commitment made in the Non-Proliferation Treaty toward slowing progress in weaponry that is central to our security. It would clearly be in the interests of both countries if such a treaty were negotiated.

A quota on missile test firings can be more readily accommodated when pressures for testing of new systems and improving existing ones are diminished by an accompanying reduction in force sizes. Therefore, a modest schedule of reductions in numbers of our major strategic systems and a diminishing quota of permitted firings of ballistic missiles to an agreed equal level for both countries are mutually supportive. They form the basis of a potential agreement that appears to be much more attractive than one based on either limitation alone.

A comprehensive approach to qualitative and quantitative restraints can include any or all of the following prime ingredients:

1. Reductions in total numbers of major strategic nuclear systems, that is, the ICBMs, the SLBMs, and the strategic bombers. One could reduce these by a factor of two or so before running into any changes in the basic assumptions of our strategic doctrine.

2. Limits on the number of new strategic systems that either country could deploy over a 10-year period.

3. Limits on the rate at which new systems could be deployed.

4. A limit on the number of flight tests of ICBMs and SLBMs carried out annually at preannounced times and over agreed test ranges.

## A Potential for Disaster

I hope that the SALT II negotiations will be completed successfully. If it proves impracticable to negotiate a more comprehensive treaty embracing both quantitative reductions and qualitative constraints on a rapid time scale, I hope that at the very least a treaty based on the Vladivostok formula will be ratified. This treaty would provide a basis for numerical reductions, hopefully to lower numbers of permitted MIRVs. It would also provide a basis on which to address the possibility of negotiating the kinds of qualitative constraints on new technology that I have described.

The experience of the SALT negotiations to date provides a strong motive for the introduction of general technological constraints, such as a missile test quota. I see this on two grounds. First, the pace of military technological progress, when funded with high budgetary priority as at present, is so fast that it inevitably outstrips diplomatic success. The negotiations so far have established quantitative limits on total numbers of missiles and strategic bombers. At the same time, however, qualitatively improved new systems enter the force, creating new problems for strategic stability.

Furthermore, there is a second problem. Looking ahead at the future prospects for arms control, we have little alternative to space satellites and remote radar surveillance as the "national technical means" allowed for verifying arms control treaties. However, as technology progresses delivery vehicles are becoming more diverse, smaller in size, and more widely based. This makes it increasingly difficult to continue as at present by formulating verifiable quantitative constraints on specified strategic systems as distinguished from tactical deployments.

For example, long-range strategic cruise missiles overlap in size with tactical weapons. The controversy over the Soviet Backfire bomber is also a case in point. Therefore whether this is or is not a favored concept of the military establishment in the United States or in the Soviet Union, general technological constraints are becoming more and more the principal tools remaining for direct limitation of the arms race.

Looking beyond the coming decade, it is becoming clear that the problems posed by a continuing qualitative arms race are dwarfed by the dangers associated with nuclear proliferation. We have very little understanding and even less agreement as to how to maintain world order when dozens of nations, many with unstable governments, acquire nuclear weapons. Our almost total preoccupation with SALT, our failure to achieve visible control and reductions, and the slow pace of progress have already robbed the United States and the Soviet Union of many opportunities to exert leadership in addressing proliferation.

These opportunities are declining. But the potential of those that remain would seem to be tightly linked to the demonstrated capacity of the two superpowers to deal effectively with their own nuclear problems. There is a real urgency to achieve visible and genuine arms control and to soon take that step toward ridding the world of nuclear weapons that President Carter spoke of in his inaugural address.

The United States and the Soviet Union must sooner or later break out of the present mold for dealing with this problem.

We must go beyond our current concern with a very detailed balancing of one another's nuclear might in order to find who's ahead. We tend to lose sight of the scale of the problem at hand: If but a tiny fraction of the enormous nuclear arsenals that we now possess, let alone those we are creating, was ever unleashed, modern civilization and mankind would suffer unprecedented disaster and unimaginable devastation.

# THE SOVIET MILITARY THREAT: RHETORIC VERSUS FACTS

## By Les Aspin

Soviet military behavior arouses considerable suspicion in the West about Russia's intentions. Behind much of this concern is the steady increase in the USSR's military efforts when U.S. force levels have fallen.

Many key elements of the Soviet defense program — spending, manpower, strategic forces, major combat equipment — have been on the rise. At the same time, many of the same indicators of U.S. military activity have held steady or fallen. The winddown from the Vietnam war high was the primary cause of the falling graph lines and accentuated the different tracks taken by the two superpowers.

Figure 1 illustrates the two opposing trends with some frequently cited examples.[1]

A glance at these trends prompts a logical question: If our efforts have declined or leveled off, why hasn't the Soviet military program slackened? Or to put the question another way: What are the Soviets up to?

We can gain some perspective on what the Russians are doing by comparing their military buildup with the buildups of others. Once we gain that perspective, we shall focus on the two crucial military issues of the day — the nuclear faceoff of the two superpowers and the conventional arms confrontation in Europe. In the nuclear realm, the key questions are whether we are better off with or without a second Strategic Arms Limitation Treaty (SALT II) and whether we can trust the Russians to abide by its terms. In the conventional realm, the key issue is how to reduce the chances of an outbreak of war in Europe.

### The Soviet Military Build-up: Rhetoric and Facts

In the ongoing debate over what the Russians are up to militarily, much attention has focused on the most alarming view — that the Soviets, using detente as a smokescreen, are striving for military superiority. To underscore the imminent danger, the proponents of this school draw a

---

*Representative Les Aspin (Dem., Wis.), a member of the House Armed Services Committee and a former Pentagon systems analyst, is perhaps the leading Congressional expert on questions involving comparisons of American and Soviet military strength.*

Figure 1. SOVIET-U.S. DEFENSE PROGRAMS,
1966-1976

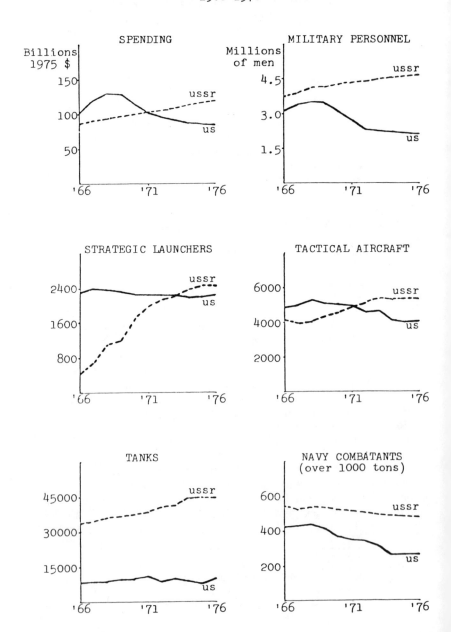

parallel between the Soviet military expansion of today and the Nazi military buildup leading to World War II.

The Committee on the Present Danger, for example, says the Soviet expansion is "reminiscent of Nazi Germany's rearmament in the 1930s."[2]

The Air Force chief of staff, Gen. David C. Jones, is more direct: "Not since Germany's rearmament in the 1930's has the world witnessed such a single-minded emphasis on military expansion by a major power."[3]

Firmer yet, Robert Heinl, a syndicated columnist and retired Marine colonel, says the Russian buildup "even exceeds Hitler's in the 1930s."[4]

Frank Barnett, director of the National Strategy Information Center, states that as a result of Russian military growth, the United States "is about where Britain was in 1938, with the shadow of Hitler's Germany darkening all of Europe."[5]

And Daniel Graham, a retired three-star general and one time director of the Defense Intelligence Agency, sees "an ominous parallel between today's reactions to the Soviet military buildup and the 1930's reaction of much of British opinion to Hitler's rearming of Germany."[6]

Shorn of the rhetoric, the individuals and groups quoted above are saying that the Soviet Union is expanding its military might at breakneck speed, just as Germany did in the 1930's. The Soviets, they say, would not necessarily even have to go to war; the overwhelming power they are about to achieve may force the West to make political concessions even without war. The Soviet and German buildups are analogous, they say, and their intentions are therefore analogous as well: they aim to present the West with an offer it can't refuse and, at the extreme, defeat the West on the battlefield if it should be so foolish as to challenge their might.

Behind the rhetoric lies the same point — a very reasonable one — that one can draw inferences about intentions by looking at *trends in capabilities*. In other words, a nation which is working at breakneck speed to expand its military capabilities, like Nazi Germany, is far more threatening than an already powerful state which is simply cruising on its existing capabilities. So one way to get a fix on Soviet intentions is to look at the trends in Soviet capabilities.

We can get one fix on those trends by displaying the dimensions of the Soviet buildup side-by-side with those of the German buildup. To widen the perspective beyond the usual comparison with the United States, it helps to show the military expansions of four other states that other commentators sometimes have found threatening. In making those comparisons here, military growth is analyzed for a five-year period. The countries and periods examined are:

- The Soviet Union, 1972-76, the most recent period for which data are available;
- Nazi Germany, 1935-39, the five years of Hitler's rule immediately preceding the start of World War II on Sept. 1, 1939. (The last German pre-war fiscal year ended March 30, 1939, so no time after the declaration of war is involved);

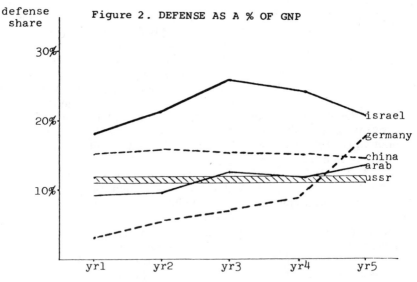

Figure 2. DEFENSE AS A % OF GNP

defense share

30%

20%    israel

germany

china

arab

ussr

10%

yr1    yr2    yr3    yr4    yr5

note: The CIA estimates Soviet military outlays at 11-12% of GNP, hence the band. This covers activities included in U.S. budget accounts, the same definition used for other nations in the chart.

- Egypt and Syria combined (labeled Arab on the charts) 1968-72, the period between the 1967 and 1973 Mideast wars;
- Israel, 1968-72, the same period as the Arab expansion;
- China, 1967-71, the main five-year period of Peking's military expansion after the Sino-Soviet split;
- North Korea, 1971-75, the most recent data covering an expansion which has received substantial attention in the United States as possibly heralding a military attack on the South.

There are two kinds of military budget expansions. In the first, a nation's military outlays increase each year because its economy is growing. In other words, a country can devote a constant percentage of its gross national product (GNP) to the military every year; but if its economy is growing, then its military budget will grow. In the second kind of expansion, the state will consciously devote a growing proportion of its GNP to the military. If it is intentions we are looking at, the latter type of expansion is usually considered more threatening. Figure 2 shows that the Germans devoted the smallest percentage of their GNP to defense at the beginning of the measurement period. The Nazi buildup entailed a concerted expansion in the proportion of the economy devoted to the military. The Soviet expansion, on the other hand, has resulted from the general growth of their economy and not because an increasing share of resources has been devoted to the armed forces.

Figures 3 through 7 show just how much the Soviets have grown in comparison with the other nations in all the major areas — money, manpower, and the main pieces of ground, sea and air weaponry. In all five cases, the Soviet buildup is the least of the lot. In terms of military budgets, Russia's grew 13 percent during the five-year period, a figure which pales beside the German growth of 868 percent and the Arab and Israeli expansion, both of which were pushing 200 percent.

When we look at naval expansions, we find that the much vaunted Russian expansion of earlier years had actually turned into a decline in the 1970's. While the Russians continued to produce large numbers of tactical aircraft, it turns out the production was only sufficient to replace their existing and aging inventory. Tank stocks rose; but only modestly.[7]

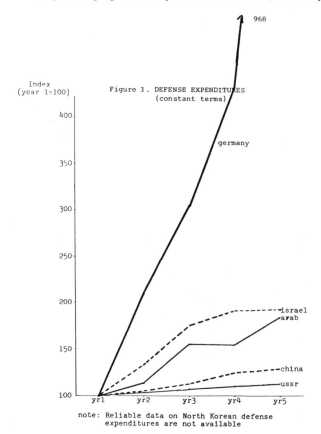

Figure 3. DEFENSE EXPENDITURES (constant terms)

note: Reliable data on North Korean defense expenditures are not available

91

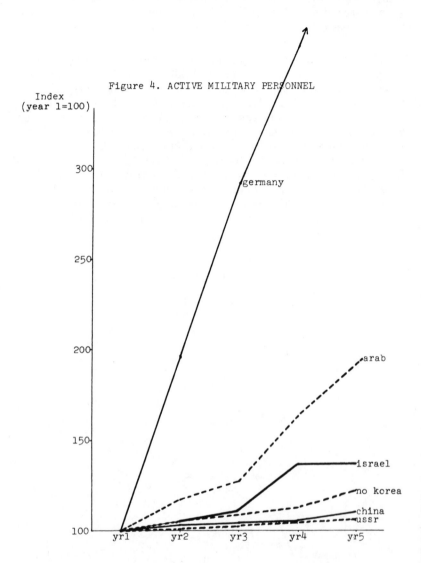

Figure 4. ACTIVE MILITARY PERSONNEL

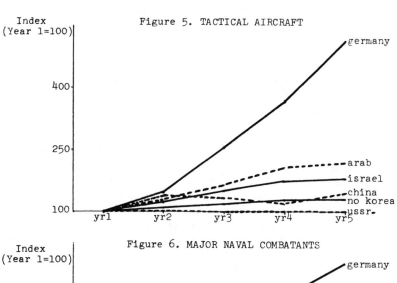

Figure 5. TACTICAL AIRCRAFT

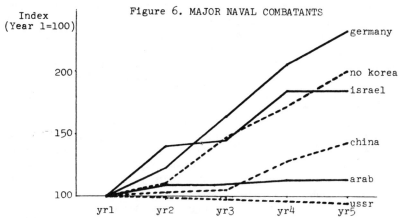

Figure 6. MAJOR NAVAL COMBATANTS

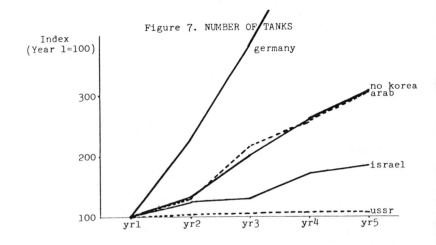

Figure 7. NUMBER OF TANKS

These are all comparisons of trends; it is the trends which many commentators have found the most threatening. It is reasonable, however, to look at the gross comparisons of the two superpowers. The key concerns are that the Soviets outspend us and outnumber us.

### The Military Budgets and Manpower

It is common these days to see it stated that the Russians outspend us militarily by 40 percent. The statistic is very true — but it is relevant only if the derivation of that number is understood. Since the Soviets do not spend dollars on defense, the intelligence agencies list what the Russians have in terms of men, tanks, planes, etc. and then calculate what it would cost to pay those people and build those weapons in the United States. By this comparision the Soviets outspent us in 1977 by about 40 percent — $130 billion to $90 billion.[8]

This system has an extreme built-in bias. The Soviets draft men and pay them less than a ruble a week. Manpower is cheap so they can afford to be profligate with it. When we use this dollar comparison, however, we figure they are being paid American military wage scales. The main reason the Soviet "dollar" budget exceeds ours is the American decision to switch to an all-volunteer force and pay uniformed personnel civilian-level wages. The absurdity of this calculation becomes evident when one considers that if we returned to the draft and the old pay scales, the U.S. defense budget would fall but the Soviet "dollar" budget would plummet even further because they have more people.

The Soviets do have far more men in uniform than this country, partly because they are so cheap. When Donald Rumsfeld was Defense Secretary he pointed out: "Soviet military manpower has grown . . . (and is) now more than double U.S. forces." The Russians have vastly more people under arms than the United States — 4.1 million versus 2.1 million.[9] The Russians have added more than 700,000 men to their forces since 1967 — and now have climbed back to the same troop level they had in the late 1950's. The expansion largely parallels the heating up of the Sino-Soviet split, and more than half of the manpower increase can be accounted for by additional troops assigned to the Sino-Soviet border, by increases in internal security forces and a growth in similar missions that do not directly threaten American interests.[10] This, of course, leaves the other half million men.

It helps to ask the fundamental question, "Just how important is it if the Russians outnumber us?" A look at the record shows this:

• The Russians outnumbered us more than two-to-one after Dwight D. Eisenhower ended the Korean war;

• The Russians outnumbered us almost two-to-one when John F. Kennedy became president;

• The Russians outnumber us about two-to-one today; and

• The only time the Russians haven't vastly outnumbered us was while we were fighting in Vietnam — and even then they still had the larger force.

Numbers don't tell the whole story, however, since they don't address the quality of manpower. For example, virtually no one in a Soviet uniform has had any combat experience; 30 percent of their recruits come from minorities that do not speak fluent Russian, the sole language in which military training courses are given; their Navy spends more time at anchor than the U.S. Navy and their airmen fly only half as many hours as ours.

### Spending for Defense

Despite all this, we cannot leap to the opposite conclusion — that the Russian military is an insignificant force posing absolutely no danger to the world today. The Russian military is certainly not fading. Soviet defense spending, while not spurting in recent years, has risen steadily for many years as shown in Figure 8.

By way of comparison, the long-term trend in the U.S. defense program is shown — using budget data since 1948 — in Figure 9. The pattern that emerges is a quantum jump in spending between the pre- and post-Korean budgets followed by a series of increases and decreases at this very high base level. Even after discounting for the Korean and Vietnam war humps, U.S. defense spending has been erratic.

The most recent decline in U.S. defense spending corresponds with our withdrawal from Vietnam. It also corresponds with SALT and detente. Many Western observers have felt that if detente were other than rhetoric to the Kremlin, Soviet defense spending should have declined in recent years like ours.

But if we put the charts on Soviet and American defense spending side-by-side, there isn't any discernible relationship. One chart might just as

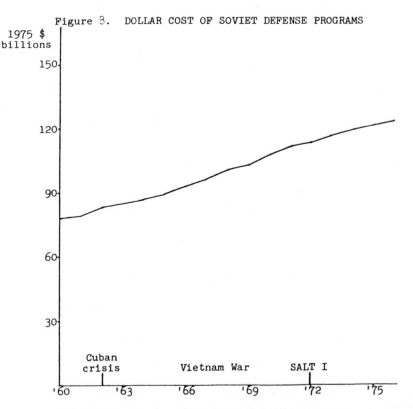

Figure 3. DOLLAR COST OF SOVIET DEFENSE PROGRAMS

well show the price of prunes in Manchuria and the other population growth in Las Vegas. Soviet spending didn't fall with ours — but it didn't rise when ours did either. This suggests there are factors driving the Soviet military budget other than the level of our activity. A few of those factors might be:

● Bureaucratic momentum — In the United States we are only beginning to realize the power of large bureaucracies to influence policies. The Soviet Union is far more bureaucratized. Its leaders, after all, come up through the governmental and party bureaucracies and owe their positions to them. One of the largest bureaucracies centers around defense production. That can help explain the consistency of Russian military outlays as opposed to the jerkiness of ours where assaults on the military-industrial complex are a regular feature of the political landscape.

● Buying military support — American political leaders do not fear a coup; Soviet leaders must live with that fear. One response can be to buy

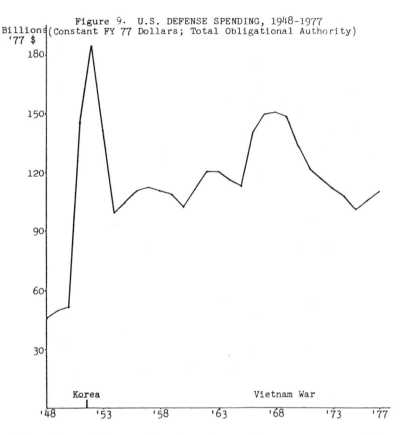

Figure 9. U.S. DEFENSE SPENDING, 1948-1977
(Constant FY 77 Dollars; Total Obligational Authority)

off the military. Slashes, such as those imposed in our country, could be destabilizing to the Soviet political system. Brezhnev may also be buying military support for SALT, a concept not unheard of in our country.

• Rupture of empire — Thirty years ago Moscow stood at the center of the communist universe. The Eastern European puppet states of that era have become increasingly more independent — and less reliable. Three decades of empire have produced two major anti-Soviet outbreaks and several minor ones. Russia finds it must occupy its western marches like the czars of old. The five occupation divisions put into Czechoslovakia in 1968 remain there today.

• Rise of China — In that same 30-year period China has been converted from a feudal state in chaos to a major power challenging Moscow both territorially and ideologically. One quarter of Russia's land and air forces are now focused on an adversary that did not exist until the 1960's.

Without a doubt Soviet power has been increasing. And it has been increasing at a time when U.S. spending on its military has been declining. If we look at what has happened to Soviet and American forces since 1968, we get a pretty frightening picture. A great gulf appears to open — a spending gap to add to the other popular gaps of recent history.

Actually the gap is caused more by a drop on our side than by a jump on theirs. And our drop is primarily, though not exclusively, the result of our winddown from Vietnam.

It is, however, this gap of recent years which gets the most attention. If we take a broader view and 1) look at what the Soviets have been doing over a greater time period, 2) look behind some of the raw data that are often quoted loosely, and 3) compare their rates of growth with those of other military powers, we get an entirely different perspective.

The individuals and groups quoted earlier were saying, in effect, if you look at what the Russians are doing, you will see they are mounting a challenge on the scale of the Nazis. We have looked at what the Russians are doing and find no such evidence. We do find that:

• The Soviets have devoted a constant level of their GNP to their armed forces for several years;

• While they have been building newer and more modern equipment, they have not been adding them to their forces at much more than the rate needed to replace aging pieces of equipment;

• The Soviets are failing to match our reduction of recent years, but they never matched our jumps of previous years;

• While reasonable men can disagree over the validity of any single kind of measurement, a variety of measures *all* show the Russian expansion to be far from dramatic. Rarely will such a broad spectrum of measurements all point in the same direction.

Contrary to the remarks of Colonel Heinl quoted earlier, the recent Russian buildup comes nowhere near "exceeding" Hitler's in the 1930's. In fact, it isn't even "reminiscent of Nazi Germany's rearmament," as stated by the Committee on the Present Danger. And as the comparisons with the Arab, Israeli, Korean and Chinese buildups show, contrary to what the Air Force chief of staff said, the Russian military expansion is not even the largest since Nazi Germany's.

No one is suggesting that the Soviet leadership is benign, docile or unthreatening. The Politburo clearly does not have the best interests of our political or economic systems at heart. But to reach the conclusion that Moscow is preparing for a confrontation is to leap beyond the evidence. Clearly, so far as Soviet intentions can be deduced from the trends in their military program, they are not as hostile as some have portayed them to be. Once we recognize this, the debate over how we should react to what the Soviets are doing can become less shrill.

The shrillness shows up in its rawest form when the nation debates its strategic arms agreements with the Russians.

## SALT II: Asset or Liability?

At this writing the SALT II treaty has not yet been completed, but the salient numerical ceilings have already been revealed. The prospective treaty has come under attack largely because it contains fewer Soviet concessions than President Carter had wanted when he issued his dramatic proposals of March 1977 and because it isn't as comprehensive as many Americans had hoped.

The crucial question, however, is not whether SALT II is less than the March 1977 proposals or less than our hearts' desire. The crucial question is whether the SALT agreement is worse than nothing. In other words, are we better off with or without SALT II?

The accords contain a series of ceilings and subceilings not only on launchers (i.e., ICBMs, bombers and submarine-launched ballistic missiles (SLBMs) combined), but also on missiles equipped with multi-headed warheads (multiple independently-targetable reentry vehicles or MIRVs) and bombers equipped with air launched cruise missiles (ALCMs). The five numerical limits that form the heart of SALT II are shown in Column 1 of Figure 10.

Figure 10. The SALT II Categories

| | (1) | (2) | (3) | (4) | (5) | (6) | (7) | (8) | (9) |
|---|---|---|---|---|---|---|---|---|---|
| | | | The United States —1985— | | | The Soviet Union —1985— | | | |
| Measure | SALT Limits | Carter/March | 1977 | With SALT | Without SALT Current Plans | 1977 | With SALT | Without SALT: Moderate | High |
| Launchers | 2160-2250 | 1800-2000 | 2059 | 1996 | 2059 | 2480 | 2200 | 3048 | 4372 |
| MIRVed msls. & ALCMd bombers | 1320 | 1100-1200 | 1046 | 1320 | 1483 | 300 | 1320 | 2036 | 2366 |
| MIRVed missiles | 1200-1250 | 1100-1200 | 1046 | 1151 | 1314 | 300 | 1224 | 1936 | 2266 |
| MIRVed ICBMs | 820 | 550 | 550 | 519 | 650 | 300 | 818 | 1398 | 1398 |
| MLBMs* | 308 | 150 | 0 | 0 | 0 | 308 | 308 | 308 | 480 |

*Modern Large Ballistic Missiles

To be sure, the SALT II numbers are higher than Carter proposed in March 1977 (See Column 2 of Figure 10). In every case, SALT II allows the Russians (and the Americans) more weapons than Carter had suggested.

Also, to be sure, the SALT II numbers require some reduction in current plans by the Americans particularly in MIRVed missiles and ALCMed bombers (See Columns 4 and 5). We have plans for 1,483 but SALT II would limit us to 1,320 — requiring a 10 percent reduction.

But the real advantage of SALT II can be seen in the last three columns.[11] In numbers of launchers and in each of the MIRVed categories, Russia's ongoing programs would give her in 1985 about half again as many pieces of equipment as SALT would hold her to (using the moderate estimate).

SALT II will marginally constrain future U.S. programs. Moscow will be much more constrained.

The counts of launchers and MIRVed weapons are simple measurements. But they are not the only measures, and, like the manpower data, they are not necessarily the best measures.

Three others are commonly used: a) the numbers of warheads-atop-missiles and bombs-inside-bombers, called force loadings; b) the megatonnage or explosive power of all those weapons; and c) the throwweight or tonnage that a missile can hurl or a bomber carry.

Figure 11 shows each of these measurements in turn, using the "moderate" estimates of Soviet forces at the end of 1985. To reflect more concretely the relative strengths and weaknesses of the superpowers, the table states U.S. strength as a percentage of Soviet strength.

Figure 11. U.S. Forces as Percentage of Soviet Forces

| Measure | 1977 | 1985 With SALT | 1985 Without SALT |
| --- | --- | --- | --- |
| Launchers | 83% | 91% | 68% |
| Force Loadings | 240% | 129% | 93% |
| Megatonnage | 35% | 29% | 24% |
| Throwweight | 75% | 51% | 37% |

The table demonstrates that no matter which of the four popular measurements of strategic power one uses, the United States comes off better with SALT II than without it.

Clearly American public opinion would not silently accept the inferiority decreed in the absence of SALT II constraints. Our efforts would be stepped up. With an eye on economy and on guaranteeing that our future without SALT would not leave us in worse shape than a future with SALT, we could push forward with several weapons systems. These could include the immediate construction of 100 FB—111 bombers and the modernization of existing ones, the retention of all Polaris subs until they reach 30 years of service (rather than the currently planned 20), deploying sea-launched cruise missiles aboard Navy attack submarines, the replacement of the remaining 450 unMIRVed Minuteman IIs with the more modern and MIRVed Minuteman IIIs, and the deployment of addisional ICBMs outside of silos.

This representative program would cost $19.9 billion in 1978 dollars to build and to operate over 10 years.

There are other programs we could pursue. For example, we could speed up the MX missile. However, if planned deployment date of 1986 is speeded up by two years, that will give no relief in the immediate future and provide very few weapons even in 1985. We could also restart the B-1 bomber program. That alternative could cost $24 billion for construction alone and be far more expensive than the program outlined here.

The effect of a $20 billion expansion program is shown in Figure 12.

Figure 12. Impact of Expansion Program

U.S. Forces as Percentage of Soviet Forces in 1985

| Measure | With SALT II | Without SALT II +$20B program |
|---|---|---|
| Total Launchers | 91% | 91% |
| Force Loadings | 129% | 125% |
| Megatons | 29% | 28% |
| Throwweight | 51% | 53% |

In other words, if we reject SALT II we can have the privilege of spending an additional $20 billion to end up in exactly the same position we would be in if we ratified SALT II.

This assumes that the Russians pursue a plausible but moderate strategic program. If the Kremlin, irate at rejection of SALT II, decided to pull out all, or even just some, of the stops, the price of playing catch-up would come still higher.

Over the years there has been a classic distinction between the Soviet and American war machines. They have produced vast hordes of weapons; we have relied on quality and felt our edge there offsets their crude numbers. In the proposed SALT II accords, we have the Russians agreeing to equality of numbers. If SALT II does not end the arms race, it would at least put an end to the numbers race and confine the competition to the qualitative area — the very area that is our strong suit. If we reject the treaty and resume the numbers race, we are entering a race in which we are already behind — surely a very curious route to choose.

### The Problem of Verification

The keystone of any Strategic Arms Limitation Treaty is our ability to be sure the Russians stick to it. Without verification, SALT is bound to collapse. But as the SALT II agreement emerges from the negotiating cocoon, charges that the Russians will seek to evade its provisions are heard.

We can divide the U.S. capability to detect violations into three broad "levels of confidence."

First, there are areas where U.S. capabilities are excellent and the possibility of cheating remote, such as the construction of more bombers or missile subs. This category includes all the areas where major violations could upset the balance of terror.

Second, there are several areas where the U.S. ability to detect violations is weak, including the addition of a handful of ICBMs or the conversion of perhaps a dozen non-bombers into bombers. In none of these cases would the violation be militarily threatening.

Third, there are two areas where there could be serious verification problems affecting any SALT III agreement in the mid-1980's: cruise missiles and the development of a new MIRV payload that would fit onto Russia's older missiles. Right now, Russia's MIRVs are so designed that they won't fit on older missiles. But if they get a transferable payload, we would have to fear that every one of their missiles was MIRVed.

We have already had a heated debate with respect to Soviet violations of the SALT I agreement. That experience has raised a number of questions about Soviet *compliance* with existing treaties, but not about our ability to *monitor* what the Soviets are doing. Indeed, the basis for allegations of violations is the detailed data we have gathered on Soviet actions since SALT I was signed. The debate has centered on what Soviet actions mean, not on what the Soviet activities have been. If the Russians had engaged in illegal behavior that had gone unnoticed, this would obviously raise doubts about our detection capabilities. But no one has even hinted that this might be the case.[12]

### Would They Try to Cheat?

The potential for undetected violations is one issue. An equally important issue, however, is whether the Soviets would attempt to cheat if they felt they could get away with it. While the potential for evasion is small, the likelihood of violations seems even more remote.

The SALT II framework provides enormous leeway for both sides to pursue strategic programs without cheating. While the Soviets without SALT II would be able to build substantially larger forces, they can still do much under treaty terms. For example, they can junk existing missiles and replace them all with more reliable and more accurate models.

There is the additional question of what benefits would accrue to the Soviet Union from cheating. There could be no political gain unless the Soviets made public their transgressions. No one is frightened by weapons they don't know exist. Yet if the Soviets did make their cheating public there would be an enormous political backlash. The U.S. government, for example, would then find itself conducting an unprecedented arms buildup in response to an incensed American public.

The dangers from Soviet violations of SALT II arise if there is a significant *military* advantage to be gained by cheating — if the Russians could cheat for a few years and then unveil a devastating superiority that would force our immediate surrender. But that is impossible. The United States under SALT II will have a very formidable strategic arsenal: almost 2,000 launchers and roughly 10,000 independently targetable warheads. To upset the balance of terror would require very large numbers indeed —

numbers that would be impossible for the Soviets to acquire without cheating on so massive and pervasive a scale as to be detectable with certainty.

What's more, they could even lose militarily by cheating. For example, one of the easier ways they could cheat undetected would be to convert to bombers about a dozen planes now used to find and destroy our subs. That would give them a miniscule increase in their retaliatory forces but at the same time punch a hole in their antisub capabilities. That's the kind of cheating we might want to encourage since we could come out ahead.

In sum, the ability to verify compliance with the accord is essential to a successful SALT agreement. But upon investigation, we find that the "problems" of verification are more imagined than real.

### The Conventional Weapons Threat

Discussions of strategic issues are in vogue. But the current stalemate in the strategic realm actually makes a conventional war more plausible: neither side dares start a nuclear war; therefore, if relations break down completely and war breaks out, there will be considerable interest by both parties in confining the fighting to conventional weaponry.

The most fearsome conventional war would be one fought in Central Europe where Soviet and American forces have faced one another for almost three decades. In Europe the issue is what we need to do to avoid being caught by a surprise Soviet attack. For years NATO planning has operated on the assumption that the Warsaw Pact would not attack until it had mobilized roughly 90 divisions near the border with West Germany. It has been estimated that these preparations would take 30 days, that NATO would detect the beginnings of this mobilization within a week and therefore have 23 days to ready itself to meet the onslaught. NATO planning has been based on mobilizing within 23 days.

The logic behind this scenario is now under frontal assault. The terms of the debate have been framed by a retired three-star Army officer, Lt. Gen. James Hollingsworth, and two U.S. senators, Sam Nunn (D-Ga.) and Dewey F. Bartlett (R-Okla.). What is envisioned is an attack by 54 Warsaw Pact divisions of such suddenness that NATO would be unaware of the preparations until 48 hours before the attack. Such a fear is based on a number of Soviet advancements over the past decade.

First, the Soviets have expanded their divisions deployed in Europe and increased their firepower. The result has been a 25 percent increase in the strength of each division. This means a more credible force in place near NATO and a reduced need for mobilization to support that force.

Second, the Soviets have increased their "organic" — within division —logistics capability. For example, they have brought into Germany a large number of trucks. Traditionally, they would have relied on vehicles from the East or confiscated from the civilian sector, obviously crimping any surprise attack strategy.

Third, there has been a rapid improvement in the quality of the Soviet tactical air force that now provides a potential for quick and very destructive strikes against key NATO sites without prior redeployment of aircraft.

Other facts used to bolster claims of a short notice attack threat are not so compelling. The most publicized of these is that NATO is vastly outnumbered across the board in men and equipment — so badly outnumbered, according to the columnists Rowland Evans and Robert Novak, that our troops in Europe are no more than "hostages." In reality, the 15 NATO nations combined spend more for defense than does the Warsaw Pact — even if we use the biased dollar comparison. In addition, NATO maintains roughly equivalent amounts of most equipment. There are some exceptions. For example, the Pact has more tanks in Central Europe while NATO has more anti-tank guided missile systems there. But overall, the quantitiative balance is not unacceptable.

Popular perceptions, however, are generally driven by charts showing large disparities that simply do not exist. For example, *Time* magazine portrayed the Warsaw Pact as having 5,300 tactical aircraft against 2,960 for NATO — an 80 percent advantage. The reality, according to then Defense Secretary James Schlesinger in his fiscal year 1975 annual report, is that each side has about 3,000 combat planes that could be used on short notice in central Europe.[13] And at every stage in the process of mobilization, NATO could deploy roughly the same number of tactical aircraft. For instance, as then Assistant Defense Secretary Leonard Sullivan told the House Armed Services Committee, each side could muster about 6,000 tactical aircraft 90 days after mobilizing.[14]

But the key question remains: how great is the likelihood of a no-notice attack?

To begin with, one must appreciate the makeup of the postulated threat.

One way to illustrate this is to consider manning levels. According to the International Institute of Strategic Studies in London, the 27 "Category I," that is, top-rated, divisions maintained by Russia's three allies in the center region are not more than three-quarters manned. If a U.S. Army division were manned at that level, it would be given the lowest rating of C-4, which means not ready. It would take months to deploy such a division.

Second, the quality of equipment in the 27 East European Pact divisions is also suspect. Most of it "trickles down" from Soviet stockpiles. Attention has focused on improvements in Soviet forces; but there has not been similar upgrading of other Pact units.

Perhaps more serious is the dubious reliability of East European divisions to support an unprovoked "bolt-out-of-the-blue" attack. Forty percent of the 54-division Pact threat is Polish or Czech. Neither of these nations can be considered a dependable ally. In fact, it is doubtful that all seven Soviet divisions in these countries would be able to abandon their occupation roles and join in an invasion.

Even if the perspective is narrowed to the 27 Soviet divisions in Eastern Europe, there are severe obstacles to a successful surprise attack. For one thing, Soviet forces are poorly deployed for an immediate offensive. U.S. officials deplore the fact that half our battalions are 50 to 100 kilometers from their places on the "front." But the average Soviet division in East Germany is 125 kilometers from the inter-German border it would have to cross.

In addition, the Soviets are still faced with a deficient logistics structure. For example, the Soviets assume relatively low ammunition expenditure rates and keep stocks that would be rapidly depleted in the intense struggle anticipated by Western analysts. Overall, the Soviets continue to be plagued by some of the same shortcomings that left their unopposed armored and mechanized division without many basic supplies on the third day of the 1968 invasion of Czechoslovakia.

Overcoming these problems would take time and would be exposed to detection. In addition there are other necessary preparations which would almost certainly be detected. In the words of former Defense Secretary Schlesinger, "The total list of potential indicators of Soviet attack in Europe is long — several hundred items."

For example, it is hard to believe that the USSR would start a ground war without a simultaneous attack at sea. To do otherwise would almost certainly concede the oceans to allied fleets and doom the "one-shot" Russian Navy which depends heavily upon striking the initial blow to deny the sea lanes to our ships. Soviet naval activity would provide early warning of an impending conflict. The Russians keep a much smaller proportion of their fleet at sea than we do. A sudden surge in deployments would tip us off.

The general and the senators not only seek to speed up our preparations in advance of war, but they also envision a wholly different scale of fighting once a war begins. General Hollingsworth argues that an attack must be stopped on the inter-German border, without trading space for time and in one-fourth the time currently anticipated.

This implies a wholesale shift of our forces in Germany since they are not stationed along the historic invasion routes of the North German Plain, but rather in south Germany in our former zone of occupation.

There is no way any nation can prepare for every threat a fertile imagination can dream up. The first task of any defense planner is to weigh probabilities against costs. A high probability threat is worth preparing for even in the face of high costs. A low probability threat may be worth preparing for when the costs are minimal. But a prudent defense planner can only conclude that redesigning the forces where the threat is minimal and the costs enormous would be a misallocation of resources. I have priced out the various proposals made by the general and the senators. They work out to $45 billion over a five-year period.[15]

Moreover, the new military strategy proposed by General Hollingsworth may actually heighten tensions and increase the likelihood of war, which certainly ought to be our goal. All military analysts, in and out of uniform, conservative and liberal, say we must judge an adversary by his known capabilities and not his unknown intentions. That applies to Soviet planners as well. What are they to think when we place a beefed up force immediately adjacent to the Iron Curtain and ready to go on 48 hours' notice?

Advocates of the Hollingsworth approach argue that it would force the Pact to mobilize before an attack, thereby giving us more warning time. But might it not induce the Pact to station more troops in Eastern Europe closer to the border and with more firepower? The end result could be two giant alliances on hair trigger status. That is hardly an improvement on today's situation.

A safer and inordinately cheaper answer is a diplomatic one. The answer is to negotiate an agreement that attempts to preclude the possibility of a surprise attack.

The mutual and balanced force reduction (MBFR) negotiations are a readily available vehicle for pursuing such an agreement. I think the following proposals are worthy of investigation.

One: Require the presence of international observers at pact and NATO installations in Central Europe.

Since a surprise attack requires extensive but observable preparations — the buildup of consumables, for example — international inspectors would help detect preparation for an attack.

Two: Restrict the number of people who can be involved in maneuvers and limit the frequency of exercises that can be held annually.

Probably the best way to disguise preparations for a no-notice assault is to hide them behind routine exercises. The Egyptians did this in 1973. Since the real danger to NATO is a massive assault, ceilings on the numbers of people involved in exercises would help prevent this.

Three: Limit the number of troops that can be rotated into Europe at any given time and mandate preannouncement of moves into the area.

An important — some say indispensable — element in the Russians' potential ability to launch an attack of sufficient size with little warning is the annual rotation by air of 100,000 troops into Central Europe over a 14-day period. These troops could be flown into Europe during what appeared to be a normal replacement program, pick up prestored weapons and become operational. This theoretical "surge" capability is substantial. By making troop substitution piecemeal, it could be effectively nullified.

### Conclusion

The rhetoric from the right tells us that the Russians are coming. The rhetoric from the left says there's absolutely nothing to worry about so we can all turn our backs on the Russians.

The truth, as usual, lies somewhere in the middle. The Soviet military is improving — learning new methods, getting more capable equipment, increasing the density of its firepower. We can shut our eyes to this only at our peril. But anyone attempting to propose a prudent policy must put the Russian developments in perspective:

- We are also learning new methods, getting more capable equipment and increasing the density of our firepower;
- The growth in Soviet military might in no way approaches the scale of other modern buildups and, in fact, pales when compared to them;
- Behind the popular quantitative measures, one must also look at quality and there we find that their forces are trained less rigorously and their equipment is generally less sophisticated;
- The slow but steady Soviet growth can be explained by concerns other than a desire to collectivize Iowa farms by force — not the least of those explanations is the growth of the Chinese challenge.

The prudent planner must, however, accept Soviet capabilities and not simply rely on guesses about Russian intentions, which could, after all, change tomorrow. But must the prudent planner's response to Soviet military programs inevitably be American military programs? Such a narrow outlook is sterile and uninspired; it guarantees only one thing — that the arms spiral will continue ever upward. This increases the likelihood of an eventual clash when we ought to be seeking means of decreasing those chances.

We ought instead to give more attention to political rather than military responses. SALT is the most obvious case. As shown here, SALT II offers the opportunity to impose *mutual* and verifiable restraints on both superpowers. SALT should be the pitchman's delight; it is the race case where we can buy more of something (in this case security) for less money.

The same is true in Europe where the alleged Soviet juggernaut is already partly shackled by unreliable allies and poor deployment. The military response gives us the chance to place both alliances on hair trigger status in Europe — hardly an improvement in security. The political approach opens up the opportunity to add some new shackles. Yes, we would have to accept more shackles as well. But surely the security of our nation, our people and our system is greater if both the eagle AND the bear are tied down than if both are loose in the same room stalking one another.

# NOTES

[1]Detailed documentation for Figures 1 through 10 can be found in Les Aspin, "What Are the Russians Up To?" (processed) Washington, D.C., November, 1977, which will appear in *International Security* (forthcoming).

[2]The Committee on the Present Danger, "What Is the Soviet Union Up To?" pamphlet, Washington, D.C., 1977, p. 10.

[3]Gen. David Jones, as quoted in Edgar Ulsamer, "The Soviet Juggernaut: Racing Faster Than Ever," Air Force Magazine, LIX (March 1976), p. 57.

[4]Col. Robert Heinl, "Soviet Leads World in Arms Outlays," Detroit News, April 7, 1976, p. 8B.

[5]Frank Barnett, as quoted in Linda Charlton, "Groups Favoring Strong Defense Making Gains in Public Acceptance," New York Times, April 4, 1977, p. 50.

[6]Lt. Gen. Danial Graham (Ret.), in United States/Soviet Strategic Options, Hearings before the Senate Foreign Relations Subcommittee on Arms Control, Oceans and International Environment, 95 Cong. 1 Sess. (1977), p. 123.

[7]Hitler began his expansion from the miniscule military force imposed by the Versailles Treaty. Therefore, displays of rates of expansion could be deceptive. The charts here do not, however, show the initial expansion after Hitler took power in January 1933. For example, the Versailles Treaty had limited the German military to 115,000 men; but by the end of 1934, it had already grown to 300,000. The higher figure is the base used in this study. Moreover, some of the largest spurts in German military growth occurred in the last year before the war, well after the German forces had reached substantial size. For instance, defense spending went from 8.2 billion to 18.4 billion reichsmarks from 1938 to 1939. Finally, most countries were devoting a smaller proportion of their resources to the military in the 1930's than is true today. In Year One for Germany (1933), she devoted 3 percent of her GNP to her armed forces. But that same year Great Britain devoted the identical proportion to her military.

[8]Central Intelligence Agency National Foreign Assessment Center, "A Dollar Cost Comparision of Soviet and US Defense Activities 1967-77," SR 78-10002, January, 1978, p. 4.

[9]Ibid., p. 12.

[10]CIA Statistics in ibid., p. 12 show a total growth of over 700,000 personnel. Intelligence estimates indicate that the Soviets have added about 300,000 men to their Far East deployments over the past decade to the current level of approximately one-half million. Similarly, 70,000 troops were added in Czechoslovakia in 1968. These two factors alone account for over half the growth.

[11]For the methodology and sources used with respect to all charts and data in this SALT section, see Les Aspin, "SALT II or No SALT," (processed) Washington, D.C., January 1978 (reprinted in the Congressional Record).

[12]For a detailed analysis of verification, see Les Aspin, "SALT Verification: Prudence & Paranoia," (processed) Washington, D.C, March, 1978 (reprinted in the Congressional Record).

[13]James Schlesinger, Annual Defense Department Report, FY 1975, Washington, D.C., March 4, 1974, pp. 87-88.

[14]Testimony on Overall National Security Programs and Related Budget Requirements, Hearings before the House Armed Services Committee, 94 Cong., 1 Sess., December 10, 1975, p. 189.

[15]See Congressional Record, March 16, 1977, pp. H 2211-2216.